Theos Friends' Progra[m]

C000186136

Theos is a religion and society think tank which seeks
opinion about the role of faith and belief in society.

We were launched in November 2006 with the suppo[rt]
Dr Rowan Williams and the Cardinal Archbishop of We[st]
Cardinal Cormac Murphy-O'Connor.

We provide

- high-quality research, reports and publications;
- an events programme;
- news, information and analysis to media companies,
  parliamentarians and other opinion formers.

We can only do this with your help!

Theos Friends receive complimentary copies of all Theos publications, invitations
to selected events and monthly email bulletins.

Theos Associates receive all the benefits of Friends and in addition are invited
to attend an exclusive annual dinner with the Theos Director and team.

If you would like to become a Friend or an Associate, please visit
www.theosthinktank.co.uk or detach or photocopy the form below, and send
it with a cheque to Theos for the relevant amount. Thank you.

Yes, I would like to help change public opinion!
I enclose a cheque payable to Theos for: ☐ **£60** (Friend) ☐ **£300** (Associate)

☐ Please send me information on how to give by standing order/direct debit

Name _____

Address _____

_____ Postcode _____

Email _____

Tel _____

Data Protection Theos will use your personal data to inform you of its activities.
If you prefer not to receive this information please tick here. ☐

By completing you are consenting to receiving communications by telephone and email.
Theos will not pass on your details to any third party.

Please return this form to:
Theos | 77 Great Peter Street | London | SW1P 2EZ
S: 97711 D: 36701

Theos – clear thinking on religion and society

Theos is a Christian think tank working in the area of religion, politics and society. We aim to inform debate around questions of faith and secularism and the related subjects of values and identity. We were launched in November 2006, and our first report *'Doing God': a Future for Faith in the Public Square,* written by Nick Spencer, examined the reasons why faith will play an increasingly significant role in public life.

what Theos stands for

In our post-secular age, interest in spirituality is increasing across western culture. We believe that it is impossible to understand the modern world without an understanding of religion. We also believe that much of the debate about the role and place of religion has been unnecessarily emotive and ill-informed. We reject the notion of any possible 'neutral' perspective on these issues.

what Theos works on

Theos conducts research, publishes reports and runs debates, seminars and lectures on the intersection of religion, politics and society in the contemporary world. We also provide regular comment for print and broadcast media. Research areas include religion in relation to public services, the constitution, law, the economy, pluralism and education.

what Theos provides

In addition to our independently driven work, Theos provides research, analysis and advice to individuals and organisations across the private, public and not-for-profit sectors. Our unique position within the think tank sector means that we have the capacity to develop proposals that carry values – with an eye to demonstrating what really works.

what Theos believes

Theos was launched with the support of the Archbishop of Canterbury and the Cardinal Archbishop of Westminster, but it is independent of any particular denomination. We are an ecumenical Christian organisation, committed to the belief that religion in general and Christianity in particular has much to offer for the common good of society as a whole. We are committed to the traditional creeds of the Christian faith and draw on social and political thought from a wide range of theological traditions. We also work with many non-Christian and non-religious individuals and organisations.

Just Money: How Catholic Social Teaching can Redeem Capitalism

Clifford Longley

Published by Theos in 2014
© Theos

ISBN 978-0-9574743-5-2

Some rights reserved – see copyright licence for details
For further information and subscription details please contact:

Theos
Licence Department
77 Great Peter Street
London
SW1P 2EZ

T 020 7828 7777
E hello@theosthinktank.co.uk
www.theosthinktank.co.uk

contents

One of the striking phenomena in the aftermath of the financial crisis is the extent of serious debate and discussion about the place of business in society. Such reflection has gone way beyond the financial sector, and there is clear evidence of a refreshing willingness on the part of many, including many business leaders, to rethink the relationship between business and society.

This publication is a very useful contribution to that discussion. It brings the distinctive insights and perspectives of its author, who is a distinguished journalist and commentator. Clifford Longley has also made a particular study of Catholic social teaching, and is an able exponent of its principles and thinking.

Catholic social teaching seeks to apply the essence of Christian moral principles to life in society. It is not an economic or political programme, but it offers a powerful way of thinking about what the common good requires, and how structures in society can promote or undermine human well being and the requirements of justice.

At the heart of many of the discussions taking place today about the place of business in society is a question of what it means to be human, and how we can best promote human flourishing. Clifford Longley ably exposes how a narrow and atrophied view of the human person as motivated purely by self-interest, has subtly pervaded much thinking about how markets work and people behave.

The truth is that to be human is to seek relationships with others founded on a true respect for their dignity, and for activities which have meaning because they serve society. These truths are well articulated by Catholic social teaching, but they are in reality universal, and also increasingly being recognised by many of all faiths and none as central to understanding what needs to change if the business world is truly to serve society, and if the culture change so urgently needed in business is to take root. This publication traces the emerging evidence of that growing consensus, and it deserves to be widely read.

Cardinal Vincent Nichols, Archbishop of Westminster

executive summary

1. Market fundamentalism, sometimes called neoliberalism, drove the world economy to the edge of the precipice in the crash of 2008. Yet it was an article of faith to market fundamentalists and neoliberal economists that this could never happen. Enormous damage – up to $30 trillion's-worth – resulted. The world was saved from even worse only by government intervention at vast expense. The public is still paying the price.

2. Neoliberalism is plainly not a scientifically sound economic theory, and economists must stop pretending it is. Critics agree the solution lies somewhere in the area of morality. The basic flaw in the system was not just about personal greed, but about the idea that free market forces need not be, and should not be, deflected by scruples about their consequences; in other words that economics has no need of morality, that "the business of business is business", and that what matters is the short-term maximisation of shareholder value.

3. Many neoliberal economists still believe that to be true, and tell politicians and business leaders that any interference in market forces is "anti-business". Despite the catastrophe of 2008, neoliberalism remains the default orthodoxy among professional economists. That means the problems have not been cured, and until they have, another catastrophe is likely. Meanwhile increased state regulation solves little, and further undermines trust.

4. Mark Carney, Governor of the Bank of England, said in the summer of 2014, "just as any revolution eats its children, unchecked market fundamentalism can devour the social capital essential for the long-term dynamism of capitalism itself."

5. One major international figure demanding fundamental change in the way the economy works is Pope Francis. He speaks from the long tradition of Catholic Social Teaching that has always been critical of market fundamentalism, in the name of those who are denied any share in its benefits.

6. Catholic Social Teaching can be traced back to ancient Greek philosophers such as Plato and Aristotle as well as to Judaeo-Christian scriptural sources. It proposes

correcting the way market forces work so that they serve the public interest and the common good. It is not anti-business, but pro-human.

7.   It offers a coherent set of principles that can protect social capital – shared values and standards such as honesty and trust – from being devoured in the way Mark Carney describes. In the long run this must be good for business as well as good for ordinary people.

8.   These principles are

    i.   prioritising the common good over profits;

    ii.   respect for human dignity and opposition to discrimination;

    iii.   sustainability, solidarity, subsidiarity and civil society;

    iv.   defence of workers' rights;

    v.   recovering a sense of vocation and virtue in pursuit of "excellence" in trade or professional skills;

    vi.   priority for the poor and disadvantaged and resistance to unfair inequality;

    vii.   importance of reciprocity and unconditional gift (gratuitousness);

    viii.   private property held under stewardship;

    ix.   dangers of marketisation and commodification;

    x.   the state's duty to protect and promote the common good.

9.   These are calls for both structural and personal change in the way the economy functions. The evidence suggests it would work much better. Neoliberalism is a false ideology that has to be confronted, in the name of sound economics and of humanity itself.

there *must* be a better way

the theory that trashed the world economy

In the autumn of 2008, as the dust settled on the wreckage of the worst financial crisis for generations, people started to ask questions about what had happened and why – including the Queen. While visiting the London School of Economics to open a new building, she asked the assembled academics, "Why did nobody notice it?" (Another version of her question was reported as, "If these things were so large, how come everyone missed them?") The "it" and "them" of her question were, of course, the signs and symptoms of an impending disaster that was about to blow a huge hole in the global financial and economic system, a hole it would take decades to repair.

The short answer to her question is because nobody thought it could happen – or nobody important enough to stop it. The International Monetary Fund was issuing reassuring messages weeks before the disaster broke.[1] Why the crisis was so unexpected has been much debated and discussed ever since, including what must be the chief point of all such inquests – could it happen again?

Modern economics is a complicated package, and there are numerous differing schools of thought. One school maintains that nothing much went amiss at the level of mainstream economic theory: it just needed to be better applied. Other voices claim that economics as a science is broken and discredited, and that it needs fundamental reform. One such voice is that of Will Hutton, economic and political commentator, who has declared that

> the dominant intellectual ideology of the last 20 years, free market fundamentalism, and the way it was applied in the financial markets, the efficient market hypothesis, was the biggest intellectual mistake this generation has ever witnessed, arguably the world has ever witnessed.[2]

Lord Adair Turner, appointed in the wake of the crisis to head the UK's Financial Services Authority, has described how

> "bad" – or rather over-simplistic and over-confident economics – helped create the crisis. There was a dominant conventional wisdom that markets were always

rational and self-equilibrating, that market competition by itself would ensure economic efficiency and stability, and that financial innovation and increased trading activity was therefore axiomatically beneficial.[3]

Similarly, Professor John Kay, who was asked by the Coalition Government to chair a review of equity markets in the light of 2008, has stated,

economists, by and large, failed to analyse or understand properly either the processes that led up to the 2007/2008 crisis or the problems that emerged from it…those in charge of economic policy were either misinformed, bemused, or both.[4]

The Governor of the Bank of England, Mark Carney, indicated his own disgust with the excesses of neoliberalism when he told a conference on Inclusive Capitalism in London in 2014:

> *Unchecked market fundamentalism can devour the social capital essential for the long-term dynamism of capitalism itself.*

My core point is that, just as any revolution eats its children, unchecked market fundamentalism can devour the social capital essential for the long-term dynamism of capitalism itself… Market fundamentalism – in the form of light-touch regulation, the belief that bubbles cannot be identified and that markets always clear – contributed directly to the financial crisis and the associated erosion of social capital.[5]

This is a formidable consensus, by no means left-wing. Indeed, many such commentators have blamed the Labour Government for being bewitched by free market ideology into thinking, in the words of Gordon Brown, that there had been an end to "boom and bust" in the national economy, and hence that "light touch" regulation of financial markets was all that was necessary.

There is much talk of "remoralising" economics, arguing that 2008 would not have happened if people had behaved better. In Pope Francis' words:

Some people continue to defend trickle-down theories which assume that economic growth, encouraged by a free market, will inevitably succeed in bringing about greater justice and inclusiveness in the world. This opinion, which has never been confirmed by the facts, expresses a crude and naïve trust in the goodness of those wielding economic power and in the sacralised workings of the prevailing economic system. Meanwhile, the excluded are still waiting.[6]

Others believe that pre-2008 mainstream economic theory, questionable though it may be in many aspects, is the best tool available until something better turns up, and can continue to throw light on economic policy-making despite the probability that the result may be misleading. Meanwhile there is still money to be made. Many of those who fall into this category, however, are deeply worried about it even as they carry on much as they have always done. The financier George Soros, for instance, in his book *The Tragedy of the European Union*, states:

> Very little has been done to correct the excess leverage in the European banking system. The equity in the banks relative to their balance sheets is wafer thin, and that makes them very vulnerable. The issue of 'too big to fail' has not been solved at all.[7]

This is reinforced by Christine Lagarde, Managing Director of the International Monetary Fund, who told the Inclusive Capitalism conference at which Mark Carney spoke:

> Progress is still too slow, and the finish line is still too far off…the too-big-to-fail problem has not yet been solved. A recent study by IMF staff shows that these banks are still major sources of systemic risk. Their implicit subsidy is still going strongly – amounting to about $70 billion in the US, and up to $300 billion in the Euro Area.[8]

These doubts rarely communicate themselves to politicians and political commentators, who continue to act as if there were an agreed and unassailable body of doctrine called 'economics' whose truth could no more be denied than the fact that the earth goes round the sun. They seem unaware that responsible economic judgements are nowadays – at least post-2008 – marked by hesitancy, because of the wide margins of error, and uncertainty, even humility, because the theory itself is suspect. The same hesitation and caution has to apply to economic predictions about future trends. Nobody really knows.

But Pope Francis hit on an important point in his reference to the "naive trust in the sacralised workings" of the free market system – that it had been advocated with an almost religious conviction as to its truth. John Kay refers to a "curious combination of ideology and mathematics" which has

> embedded in a broader view of the economic world that lauds the equilibration and efficient character of markets. It has provided intellectual support for market fundamentalism and helped shift prevailing political thought rightwards. The economic determinism and love of simple, all-embracing explanation of complex events – for so long characteristic of the political left – are today equally, or more fervently, embraced on the right.[9]

His reference to "fervour" is revealing. The advocacy of free market economics has sometimes taken on the attributes of a moral crusade.

when self-correction fails

One undeniable change, which makes life much more difficult post-2008, is the decline of trust – trust in those with whom one does business, but also trust in the reliability of the whole economic process. Through this decline in trust, risk assessment has become more difficult. This is one of the fundamental reasons why medium and small businesses have found it so hard to get credit. Lending institutions have lost confidence in their ability to work out who is creditworthy. They no longer trust their computers to know best.

For the previous 30 years, financial and business practice had followed economic theory in the belief that the freer markets were of government intervention, the better they delivered the goods. Crucial to that assumption was the conviction that, though markets could sometimes get themselves into various difficulties, they could be relied upon to get themselves out again. In short, painful though the process sometimes was, markets were self-correcting. This theory, or group of related theories, is variously called 'neoliberalism', 'neo-classical economics', 'the Washington Consensus' (because of its history), 'laissez faire', 'market fundamentalism' or 'market triumphalism' (by its critics), or just mainstream economics, the name preferred by those who do not consider there are credible alternatives. David Harvey defines neoliberalism as:

> a theory of political economic practices that proposes that human well-being can best be advanced by liberating individual entrepreneurial freedoms and skills within an institutional framework characterised by strong private property rights, free markets, and free trade. The role of the state is to create and preserve an institutional framework appropriate to such practices... Furthermore, if markets do not exist in areas such as land, water, education, healthcare, social security, or environmental pollution then they must be created, by state action if necessary. But beyond these tasks the state should not venture.[10]

Implicit in this definition is the notion that neoliberal economic systems are self-correcting, and any destructive tendencies they exhibit, self-limiting. The record of events from 2007 onwards shows increasing levels of alarm in financial circles that this was no longer proving true. The final shock came early in the morning on 15th September 2008 when, after months of financial turmoil, America's fourth largest investment bank, Lehman Brothers, filed for bankruptcy. Advocates of the process of "creative destruction", the supposed process by which markets self-correct by weeding out the weaker players, never envisaged a failure on this scale. Lehman Brothers had assets of $600 billion: it was the largest bankruptcy in world history.

Such was the interdependency of global finance, Lehman's failure was an immediate and dire threat to many other financial institutions, large and small, and not just in America. People close to the action realised that they could all go bankrupt. It was easy to imagine what the result would look like short-term, impossible to imagine it long term. Cash machines all over the world would cease to work, bank branches would have to close their doors to hold at bay angry crowds demanding to withdraw their savings. Businesses, unable to function without day-to-day finance and with their cash reserves wiped out, would come to a halt and quickly face ruin. Entire populations would be thrown out of work.

Lehman's downfall was also part of a previous chain reaction, a key element of which was the issuing of property mortgages on a massive scale to people who could ill afford them – so-called "sub-prime" mortgages. They were more risky, but financiers attempted to reduce the risk by spreading it more widely. Ultimately, however, that merely increased the pool of people who would lose money when the mortgages proved unsustainable.

When the second act of the drama started to unfold, it was no longer possible to pretend that markets were self-correcting. Far from functioning best with the minimum of government intervention, that intervention now became absolutely essential if the whole house of cards was not to collapse and bring down the national economies of countries across the globe.

Governments stepped in to prop up the global banking system. The collapse of Lehman's had to be the last domino to fall: the rest were "too big to fail". It was the nemesis of creative destruction and the end, too, of government non-intervention. Henceforth governments would need to give close attention to the internal affairs of banks, how they were managed and by whom. And henceforth governments would have to do what market forces had failed to do. The economics of banking, and large parts of the economy in other sectors, would be permanently distorted by the knowledge that governments, with their theoretically unlimited capacity to lend or print money, were the real bearers of ultimate risk, not the businesses concerned and their shareholders.

Companies were said to have "privatised their profits, but nationalised their losses." The notion of "moral hazard" – that those who took undue risks would eventually have to pay the price – was no longer valid. Yet moral hazard is a crucial balancing factor in the working of free markets, where profit margins and risk are inseparably connected. A market where risk is being borne by governments, not by shareholders, cannot be called a free market. It can scarcely be called capitalism.

Even with expensive rescue packages in place, the damage to the world economy was still enormous. Government intervention came at a high price. For instance, taking major British banks including RBS and HBOS into partial public ownership cost the British Government some £123.93 billion.[11] At the time, RBS was the world's largest bank.

It is not hard to see why it was necessary. Their bankruptcy would have wiped out assets worth ten times as much. With this direct intervention came huge secondary costs. The National Audit Office estimated that the total cost of support for the British financial sector had reached £850 billion – which it nevertheless judged as "justified" by the need to head off the potential damage of one or more of them going under, and to preserve people's savings and confidence in the financial system.[12] The cost became a debt the British Government had to borrow, pay interest on, and eventually repay. It destabilised the British economy and wrecked the public finances, already under strain. It hit the British taxpayer hard.

Similar effects were felt in America. The US Government Accountability Office estimated that the crisis cost the American economy more than $22 trillion, though calculated on a different basis.[13] Globally, there have been many estimates of the total cost of the crisis, and there is uncertainty as to how much of the subsequent crisis in the Eurozone can be regarded as fall-out from 2008 and therefore added to the total, or regarded as having been caused by other structural weaknesses. But as a crude figure a global cost of $30 trillion would not be an unreasonable estimate.

In Britain, not only had the "nationalisation of bankers' losses" placed a burden of debt on the shoulders of every citizen, but the contraction of economic activity caused a rise in unemployment, pushing up the cost of unemployment pay and other forms of welfare benefit, and reducing the total amount of income tax being collected. The slowing down of the British economy as a result of the 2008 crisis has cost vast amounts, and continues to do so, in lost earnings and investments. The economist David Blanchflower has calculated that real wages went down by between 8 and 10 per cent as a result of the 2008 crisis.[14] This was long-term damage, wealth that will never be recovered.

is there no alternative?

So far, efforts to rebuild the free market system on a more secure basis have made slow progress. What holds them back is the lack of an alternative economic theory to replace neoliberalism, which continues to exercise a hold over the imaginations of many economists because of its elegant simplicity and promise of mathematical certainty. The book *What's the Use of Economics?*, edited by Diana Coyle, Director of Enlightenment

Economics, summarised the dilemma facing those trying to teach the next generation of economists thus:

> The gap between important real-world problems and the work-horse mathematical model-based economics being taught to students has become a chasm. Students continue to be taught as if not much has changed since the crisis, as there is no consensus about how to change the curriculum.[15]

Many commentators have pointed out this lack of a clear alternative, including Alan Greenspan, former chairman of the US Federal Reserve, who was widely regarded as the father of modern free market economics and is one of its best known and most admired practitioners.

In his latest book *The Map and the Territory*, Greenspan has a section at the end headed 'THERE *MUST* BE A BETTER WAY', (in capitals) where he notes the interdependence of economics and politics, part of the larger relationship between economics, and cultural and moral values. "Our highest priority going forward," he says, speaking specifically of America, "is to fix our broken political system. Short of that, there is no viable long-term solution to our badly warped economy."[16] In other words, whatever the solution is, it is not to be found in free market economics. It lies instead, he suggests, in a shared system of values. "Democratic societies such as ours require a broad and deep adherence to a set of principles that are not subject to compromise." For Americans, that is supplied by the Bill of Rights enshrined in the American Constitution.

Until September 2008, Greenspan's preferred economic theory was hardline free market. He was a fan of Ayn Rand, the American novelist and philosopher who took libertarianism, both in economics and in life, to its limits. Indeed in many ways he was her successor. He had been a member of her inner circle, the Ayn Rand Collective, and a leading proponent of her philosophy called Objectivism. She was by his side on public occasions. She took her dislike of altruism and collectivism to the point where she asked her followers to swear never to commit an unselfish act.

At that time, Greenspan's model of the person who engaged in pure *laissez faire* economic activity went by the name of *Homo economicus*, Economic Man. Economic Man is assumed always to act on a purely rational calculation – based on full knowledge of all relevant factors – of his own self-interest. Such an "ideal" economic actor was at the heart of mainstream economic theory, on which all economic predictions were based and round which all mathematical models were designed. But after the shock of 2008, which all models failed to predict, Greenspan began to look for factors other than rational self-interest that might motivate human conduct in the market place. His hope was that ultimately a better understanding of human nature might enable better economic models to be constructed, which worked.

His interest lay in the possibility of replacing the assumed rationality of *Homo economicus* with something closer to real life, recognising that economic decisions could be affected by irrational herd behaviour – the human desire not to be out of step with the crowd – and by a range of emotional influences such as those that are studied in the relatively new field of behavioural economics. Thus could economics claim back its status as an objective science, in which the ability to predict future outcomes accurately was essential.

The desire of economists to have their subject accepted as a science has been described by one of their number as "physics envy" – an ironic reference to the Freudian theory about subconscious penis envy.[17] Physics is a genuinely pure science. Meteorology, for instance, is based on it. But while two meteorologists may disagree about what the weather might do the following day, they both know that the more facts they (or their computers) can take into account, the better their predictions will be. Economists want their subject to be similarly predictive. But they don't know what to program into their computers, or whether human behaviour is even capable of being reduced to a set of scientific laws.

There are many instances where the outcome of an economic policy has proved to be opposite to what was expected.[18] This highlights an obvious flaw in neoliberal economic theory: the assumption that the level at which an item is priced in a perfectly rational market reflects in a highly condensed form everything that can be known about the supply and demand for that item, hence prices in such a market are literally infallible. They cannot be wrong. It is on this basis that neoliberals dismiss any proposals from government or elsewhere that look like an interference in market price-setting, for instance in relation to energy or housing. But in practice the knowledge possessed by markets is always imperfect, and behaviour in markets is often not rational. The price set by a market takes no account of externalities, such as the social costs of a housing shortage which can translate into demands on the taxpayer for subsidies or welfare benefits. Nor does the theory take account of herd behaviour, and the tendency of markets to be governed not by rational choice but by panic or exuberance. And it ignores the natural tendency to rig markets by creating formal and informal cartels – which Adam Smith famously called a "conspiracy against the public."[19]

Among the factors Greenspan identified that could change economic behaviour apart from rational self-interest was morality. "No human being can avoid the imperative of judging right from wrong," he declared:

> What we feel is right and just reflects our own deep-seated code of values. We rationally codify our introspective view of how our actions will further our values

and, therefore, what set of actions we believe, rightly or wrongly, will nurture our lives. The value systems of most people are rooted in religion and culture.[20]

This is strange talk for a free market economist, for the whole point of economics being a pure science was to liberate it from the domain of moral values – to deny that morality had any business judging economic outcomes, or indeed any role in economics at all, any more than it did in physics. Ayn Rand represented the extreme case. She had published a collection of essays under the provocative title *The Virtue of Selfishness* in which she rejected altruism and applauded egoism as an ethical ideal.[21] The rational self-interest of *Homo economicus* was right: this was not just how things were, but how they ought to be. Considerations of what is or isn't fair just didn't come into it. Yet here is Greenspan again, writing, in the light of 2008:

> Most people in a society or country tend to hold similar standards of fairness. This in democratic societies ultimately determines what is legally 'just,' the basis for our set of laws. Such fundamental beliefs are the major glue that holds societies together.[22]

In the American context, Greenspan's reference to religion and culture is an implicit acknowledgement of the presence within that culture of what are termed Judaeo-Christian moral values, which represents the coming together of overlapping traditions – Protestantism, Catholicism, and Judaism, but with a strong influence also of the Enlightenment.

On behalf of one such tradition, Pope Benedict XVI gave his response to the 2008 financial crisis in his encyclical letter *Caritas in Veritate*, published in 2009.[23] Like Greenspan, he stressed that business leaders can no longer ignore the effect of their activities on the social context in which they operate. Yet the short-term maximisation of shareholder value guarantees the exclusion of all considerations based on the "common good" – a concept discussed in more detail later, which in this context means something similar to "a commitment to the public interest". Pope Benedict wrote:

> One of the greatest risks for businesses is that they are almost exclusively answerable to their investors, thereby limiting their social value... There is nevertheless a growing conviction that business management cannot concern itself only with the interests of the proprietors, but must also assume responsibility for all the other stakeholders who contribute to the life of the business: the workers, the clients, the suppliers of various elements of production, the community.

Professor Kay, in an address to a *Blueprint for a Better Business* conference in 2013, contrasted two statements from the annual reports of ICI, which was in 1987 Britain's largest industrial company.[24] Its report for that year contained the following statement of intent:

> ICI aims to be the world's leading chemical company serving customers internationally through the innovative and responsible application of chemistry and related science. Through the achievement of our aim we will enhance the wealth and well-being of shareholders, employees, customers, and communities which we serve and in which we operate.

By 1994, a radical overhaul of ICI's business strategy had taken place, and its annual report for that year amended the company's purpose to this:

> Our objective is to maximise value for our shareholders by focusing on businesses where we have market leadership, a technological edge, and a world competitive cost base.

So employers, customers and communities had been eliminated as objects of ICI's direct concern, except in so far as they affected profitability.

Professor Kay commented that "the difference between these two statements is the issue we ought to be debating." He said the change, which prioritised short-term objectives like enhancing shareholder value over long-term ones like research and development, was largely responsible for the eventual demise of ICI.

how a bank became a monster

Cultural change in British business, for better or worse, often originates with the feeling that "they do things better in America," usually accompanied by the perception that traditional British thinking is sclerotic and out-of-date. The internal transformation in ICI may have been of that type, and it certainly affected the financial sector.

This shines through from the analysis of the phenomenal success, followed by disastrous failure, of the Royal Bank of Scotland in 2008, given in Iain Martin's book *Making it Happen*.[25] Martin focuses on Sir Fred Goodwin's predecessor George Mathewson, who graduated from St Andrews in maths and physics, and went to America from Scotland as part of the 1960s brain drain.

"It was a revelation," Martin describes. "In contrast to the 1960s Scotland, America seemed invigorating, exciting and open to change, a country where a young engineer could glimpse the possibilities of wealth creation." He later returned to Scotland as a successful businessman, and joined RBS at a crucial moment.

> Highly energetic, blunt and magpie-like in his enthusiasm for new ideas and technical innovation, he was far removed from the traditional image of the cautious Edinburgh banker. The Royal Bank seemed slow, staid and lacking in sophistication. Profits were measly.

The bank really is in trouble, Mathewson thought.

> The more he saw it from the inside the more he believed a total transformation of structures and culture, led by him of course, was required.[26]

By 1996, the transformation was complete and the Royal Bank of Scotland was a very different company. Branch offices had been closed, old-fashioned bank managers dispensed with, decision-making concentrated on head office. Soon, profits started to boom. "But a 'sales culture' had been created," writes Martin, "with many employees in the bank now measured according to rigorous targets dictating how much they must sell in the way of products to customers." He reports one executive remarking, "We created a monster":

> The basic business of banking and the public's understanding of it were being altered. Customers used to thinking in terms of asking nicely for credit started to find the banks were competing to give them more credit than perhaps they needed, and trying to sell products… [27]

This kind of radical change, stimulated by the 1986 Big Bang when the financial sector in Britain was deregulated, happened at varying speeds across much of the banking industry and financial sector, but it was to leave nothing undisturbed.

Why did it happen?

chapter 1 – references

1   See the evaluation report, *IMF Performance in the Run-Up to the Financial and Economic Crisis: IMF Surveillance in 2004-07*, para. 43 at page 17: "IMF staff was essentially in agreement with the views of the US, UK, and other advanced country authorities that their financial systems were essentially sound and resilient." http://www.ieo-imf.org/ieo/files/completedevaluations/crisis-%20main%20report%20(without%20moises%20signature).pdf

2   Will Hutton, 'Thanks to the credit crunch all bets are off' *The Guardian*, 27 February 2009 http://www.theguardian.com/commentisfree/video/2009/feb/27/will-hutton-capitalism-crisis

3   Adair Turner, *'Economics, conventional wisdom and public policy'*, Institute for New Economic Thinking, Inaugural Conference, Cambridge, April 2010; http://ineteconomics.org/sites/inet.civicactions.net/files/INET%20Turner%20%20Cambridge%2020100409.pdf

4   John Kay, 'Circular Thinking', *RSA Journal*, Issue 4, 2013; http://www.thersa.org/fellowship/journal/archive/issue-4-2013/features/circular-thinking

5   Mark Carney, 'Inclusive Capitalism: Creating a sense of the Systemic', www.bankofengland.co.uk–/publications/Pages/speeches/default.aspx 2014.

6   Pope Francis Apostolic *Exhortation Evangelii Gaudium* par 54.

7   George Soros *The Tragedy of the European Union: Disintegration or Revival?* PublicAffairs (NewYork, 2014 and Kindle): Part 1, Summer 2013, Third Interview, Markets.

8   Christine Lagarde *Economic Inclusion and Financial Integrity* www.imf.org/external/np-/speeches/2014/052714.htm 2014.

9   John Kay, 'Circular Thinking', op. cit.

10 David Harvey *A Brief History of Neoliberalism* (Oxford University Press, 2005, and Kindle): Introduction.

11 National Audit Office *The Financial Stability Intervention* 2012.

12 National Audit Office *Maintaining financial stability across the United Kingdom's banking system* 2009.

13 United States Accountability Office *Financial Crisis Losses* 2013: output losses $13 trillion, housing equity losses $9 trillion.

14 David Blanchflower Vox website http://www.voxeu.org/article/falling-real-wages-uk 2014.

15 Diana Coyle (ed.) *What's the Use of Economics?: Teaching the Dismal Science After the Crisis* (London Publishing Partnership, 2012), page ix.

16 Alan Greenspan *The Map and the Territory: Risk, Human Nature, and the Future of Forecasting* (Allen Lane, 2013, and Kindle), p. 302.

17 'Economists Suffer from Physics Envy' *Bloomberg Businessweek Magazine* (19 February 2006) http://www.businessweek.com/stories/2006-02-19/online-extra-economists-suffer-from-physics-envy .

18 For instance Jeremy Warner commented that "markets have reacted to the forward guidance in the opposite way to the one you might expect" ('Inflation will be back', *Daily Telegraph* 8 August 2013).

19 Adam Smith *The Wealth of Nations* (1776) "People of the same trade seldom meet together, even for merriment and diversion, but the conversation ends in a conspiracy against the public, or in some contrivance to raise prices".

20 Alan Greenspan *The Map and the Territory: Risk, Human Nature, and the Future of Forecasting* (Allen Lane, 2013).

21 Ayn Rand *The Virtue of Selfishness* (New American Library, 1964).

22 Alan Greenspan *The Map and the Territory*.

23 Pope Benedict XVI *Caritas in Veritate* 2009.

24 John Kay *What is the Business Need for Change?* www.blueprintforbusiness.org/–content/ download/43994/340981/file/BBB%20Conference%202013%20-%20Pamphlet.pdf 2013.

25 Ian Martin *Making it Happen: Fred Goodwin, RBS, and the men who blew up the British economy* (Simon and Schuster, 2013).

26 Ibid. p.

27 Ibid. p.

a "dirty little secret"

when economics forgot what it was for

The post-2008 Greenspan is not alone in wanting economics to operate in the real world. The award winning *Financial Times* journalist Gillian Tett, one of the few to warn of an impending financial disaster ahead of the event, said in the final chapter of her book *Fool's Gold* that her training as an academic anthropologist had taught her that "nothing in society ever exists in a vacuum or in isolation."[1] It was the neglect of that truth which "cuts to the very heart of what has gone wrong" in the world of finance and economics. Like the author of this report, not being an economist rescues her from membership of one of the various schools into which economics has become divided. Without the baggage of an academic education in university economics, it is easier to be dispassionate when other people's ideological sacred cows are candidates for the slaughter house.

Like Alan Greenspan, she said she was still "trying to make sense of the last decade of grotesque financial mistakes." In recent years, she noted,

> regulators, bankers, politicians and investors and journalists have all failed to employ truly holistic thought – to our collective cost. Bankers have treated their mathematical models as if they were an infallible guide to the future, failing to see that these models were based on a ridiculously limited set of data… The only thing that is more remarkable than this deadly state of affairs was that it went unnoticed for so long.

Millions of ordinary families, Tett pointed out, have suffered shattering financial blows. "They are understandably angry. So am I. It is a terrible damning indictment of how twenty-first century Western society works." In essence, what is now needed, she states, "is a return to the seemingly dull virtues of prudence, moderation, balance and common sense."[2] She has, as it were, felt her way intuitively back to Plato and to two of his four cardinal virtues, omitting – we can assume unintentionally – courage and justice. Other writers, whose work will be discussed later, have come to not dissimilar conclusions.

The prominent British economics commentator Anatole Kaletsky states in his book *Capitalism 4.0*:

> During and after the crisis, academic recommendations from the left and the right differed in almost every respect apart from one striking feature – a theoretical detachment from reality that made them almost completely useless in practice. One of the dirty little secrets of modern academic economics, for example, is that the computer models used by central banks and finance ministries to guide them in setting interest rates and regulating banks say almost nothing about finance... Politicians and central bankers turning to academic economists for guidance in the financial crisis were effectively told: "you are on your own since the situation you have to deal with is impossible – our theories show it cannot exist".[3]

This brings us to a serious problem in post-2008 economics. As Greenspan, Tett, Kaletsky and others agree, by any standards except its own, free market economics had behaved disastrously. In aid of short-term profit, many institutions in the financial sector had put aside all moral considerations, or where those considerations were expressed in regulatory principles and practices, had successfully pressed governments to strip away all but the minimum statutory checks on financial conduct. Where, despite this "regulatory capture", such minimal checks were still in place they often ignored them, legally or illegally. *Homo economicus,* typically the man at a desk on the trading floor, had seen his humanity reduced to that of an amoral automaton, programmed to pursue only his rational self-interest – in his case expressed as bonuses in reward for profits made. His entire *raison d'être* was to be driven by generous incentives to make as much money as possible as fast as possible.

Dominic Barton, Global Managing Director, McKinsey & Company, referred in a speech to the Blueprint for a Better Business conference in 2012 to "top teams working overtime to meet near-sighted targets – and they are blind to the impact of their actions on any broader measure of value."[4] Individuals, he said, "have lost sight of the broader goals of a free-market economy." Adam Smith described capitalism as the mechanism by which "a general plenty diffuses itself through all the different ranks of society." Yet individuals, like businesses, Barton continued, "have shifted to view their economic actions as an exercise in maximising one's personal wealth – an activity devoid of serving a higher goal."

It is unfair, perhaps, to dismiss this as simply the "creed of greed", the proposition made famous by the character Gordon Gekko in the 1987 Hollywood film *Wall Street*. "Greed, for lack of a better word, is good," he declared.

Greed is right. Greed works. Greed clarifies, cuts through, and captures, the essence of the evolutionary spirit. Greed, in all of its forms; greed for life, for money, for love, knowledge, has marked the upward surge of mankind and greed, you mark my words, will not only save Teldar Paper, but that other malfunctioning corporation called the USA.

There is the ghost of Ayn Rand behind those remarks.

money, war and justice?

A soldier on the battlefield who desires to kill as many of the enemy as possible is not necessarily a psychopath. He is a cog in a larger wheel, and the ultimate point of the army machine in which he plays his part may be to make peace, defend the innocent or correct rampant injustice. Wars can be just. That is to say they can be a means to justice, fought justly. The tradition in Western ethics, derived from patristic and medieval Christian philosophy but with connections to Jewish and Islamic thought, sets out the conditions under which killing in battle is morally permissible. It is not permissible, for instance, to kill civilians or wounded enemy soldiers, or prisoners of war, or more of the enemy than necessary. Working on the trading floor of a large investment bank in order to make money can equally be morally permissible under the right conditions. But there needs to be an equivalent set of conditions and principles, an ethical doctrine of Just Money, to set limits and guide behaviour. It is the search for these principles that gives the present report its title.

As Just War theory can protect a soldier from moral and psychological harm when making war in battle, so a Just Money theory can protect a financial trader from being personally harmed by what he does, making money in the City. Both making war and making money are morally dangerous. In the latter case, the consequence of a chaotic and hedonistic lifestyle, and eventually personal destruction, is explored in the post-2008 film, set pre-2008, *The Wolf of Wall Street*. This journey, from making money to self-destruction, is also dramatized in the novel *The Bonfire of the Vanities* by Tom Wolfe, later made into a movie of the same name. Both films emphasise the hubristic arrogance that can accompany the high rewards of financial trading, especially when it is supported by an ideology. An ideology is not a conscious belief in a worldview regularly and deliberately renewed, but more like a pattern in the cultural wallpaper, unquestioned, just 'what everybody knows is the case.'

There is one other relevant product of Hollywood which points in a different direction, and it is found, perhaps surprisingly, in the major sub-plot of the 1990 film *Pretty Women*. A hot-shot lawyer and financier arrives in town to buy out an old, established shipbuilding company that has fallen on hard times. He is an asset-stripper who knows the company owner has little choice but to sell, even though it means closing the business with all that will follow for the employees and the wider community. But his hard *Homo economicus* heart is melted by the love of a good woman. Having gone through a moral crisis he decides to save the shipyard and go into partnership with the owner, to invest in it and build more ships. He tells the owner

> My interests in your company have changed. I no longer wish to buy your company and take it apart. But I don't want anyone else to, either. And it is still extremely vulnerable. So I find myself… in unfamiliar territory. I wanna help you. I think we can do something very special with your company.[5]

Thus the film subtly presents the two faces of American capitalism: rapacious, impatient and greedy on the one hand, constructive, long-term and working for the common good on the other. And the former steps in to save the latter. Non-economists, of course, think the film is mainly about sex.

rational self-interested choice

Both Alan Greenspan and Gillian Tett describe a world in which high finance operated behind a wall, or within a cocoon, within which economic principles ruled supreme. The efficient market hypothesis, for instance, regarded free markets as almost magical devices for adjusting supply and demand, and hence prices, to reach a state of stable equilibrium that could not be bettered by human intervention. In other words, while market forces were in one sense blind and dumb, in another sense they were all-seeing and all-knowing. They could safely be left to produce the most efficient outcome.

Rational choice theory predicts that individuals act to balance costs against benefits, to make economic decisions that maximize their personal advantage. Both these economic principles presuppose that *Homo economicus,* if not a perfect model of human nature, is close enough. Close enough, anyway, for clever computer programmers to write programs that will replicate human behaviour in the market place. "Rational self-interest" is easily programmable in a mathematical model – you simply have to tell the computer to compare two outcomes and choose the larger – which can be regarded as both rigorous and internally consistent, thus satisfying two of the main criteria of acceptability in free market economic theory.

The most obvious challenge to these assumptions is that they do not correspond to how people actually behave in real life, outside the cocoon within which economics operates. Indeed, it has been pointed out that many of the people who spend time within the cocoon do return to real life, for instance when they go home to their families every evening. There values are different. They live divided lives.

One major study to identify and name this phenomenon came about through collaboration between the Vatican and the John A. Ryan Institute for Catholic Social Thought of the Center for Catholic Studies at the University of St Thomas, Minnesota.[6] Prepared with the aid of business people, it struck a chord in many business and professional circles. It stated that

> obstacles to serving the common good come in many forms – lack of rule of law, corruption, tendencies towards greed, poor stewardship of resources – but the most significant for a business leader on a personal level is leading a 'divided' life.

The phenomenon is easily observed and commonly experienced. It was mentioned by Mark Carney in the speech already mentioned when he said,

> financiers, like all of us, need to avoid compartmentalisation – the division of our lives into different realms, each with its own set of rules. Home is distinct from work; ethics from law; the individual from the system.[7]

An individual in this situation feels it is necessary to take on a different personality on entering the workplace, with a narrower set of values from those which apply outside. It is commonly described as the need to "leave personal baggage at the door" – in other words, to shake off cultural imperatives and social assumptions within which people live their ordinary lives, for instance in families or in various social activities, in order to become *Homo economicus,* motivated purely by rational self-interest, in the office. The sensation of becoming such a person is frequently described as an uncomfortable or troubling one, made easier to bear by the company of other individuals with the same experience, and also by the assumption that it is justified, as being necessary for the performance of certain professional duties.

divided life or common good

This description of the divided life proposes as an antithesis – as the presumed opposite of the rational self-interest of *Home Economicus* – the principle of the common good. What does this mean? It clearly goes beyond saying that economics and finance cannot function without moral values. It is more subversive of standard economic doctrine than that, raising fundamental questions, for example, about the philosophical and cultural underpinning of modern economics, both mainstream (or neoliberalism) theory and the opponents of mainstream theory. Both sides of that argument concentrate on the word "rational" in the phrase "rational self-interest", and on the word "interest." Rational in this context means unmoved by emotion or any other influence not strictly based on the evidence, including morality. There is debate, for instance, about whether the definition of "rational" is set too narrowly – whether it is rational, when trading in a market, to move with the herd, say, because the herd may know something one doesn't. The assumptions behind "interest" are to do with personal advantage, over and against advantage to others. The touchstone often cited is a phrase from Adam Smith's *The Wealth of Nations*,

> It is not from the benevolence of the butcher, the brewer, or the baker, that we can expect our dinner, but from their regard to their own interest. We address ourselves not to their humanity but to their self love.

By "humanity" Smith is referring to their finer feelings, the humanitarian impulse.

This apparent put-down to the notion of benevolence is actually uncharacteristic of Smith's generally high moral tone, not only in *The Wealth of Nations* but in his earlier work *The Theory of Moral Sentiments,* where he heaps the highest praise on the person who has sympathy for the plight of others. He says in his *Theory of Moral Sentiments*,

> how amiable does he appear to be, whose sympathetic heart seems to re-echo all the sentiments of those with whom he converses, who grieves for their calamities, who resents their injuries; and he rejoices at their good fortune!

This warm human spirit is often neglected by those who know Smith only through his *Wealth of Nations*, or through reductions of it in economic textbooks. Clearly he is not in the Ayn Rand camp.

the "invisible hand"

Smith's belief in the benefits of pursuing self-interest is expressed in his famous reference to the invisible hand, which has become the foundational metaphor of free market economics. Writing of a hypothetical businessman who exercises a preference for home-grown produce, he says:

> Preferring the support of domestic to that of foreign industry, he intends only his own security; and by directing that industry in such a manner as its produce may be of the greatest value, he intends only his own gain; and he is in this, as in many other cases, led by an invisible hand to promote an end not part of his intention. Nor is it always the worse for the society that it was no part of it.

> By pursuing his own interest, he frequently promotes that of the society more effectually than when he really intends to promote it. I have never known much good done by those who are affected to trade for the public good.[8]

In other words, he doesn't shun foreign produce because he is patriotic – "trading for the public good" – but because it is more profitable to do so – "intending only his own security." As a result he is unwittingly – "led by an invisible hand" – to contribute to the national economy.

> *The notion of the invisible hand has been used to elevate free market economics to an almost mystical level.*

The notion of the invisible hand has been used to elevate free market economics to an almost mystical level, hinting that a benevolent Providence watches over market forces to ensure an outcome which is always to the general benefit. This ignores Smith's own qualification expressed by the word "frequently", which clearly conveys he had no intention of propounding a general law. But the invisible hand hypothesis, which this passage gave rise to, also acquits those engaged in economic processes of having any responsibility towards the common good beyond that of making a private profit. This is directly echoed in a seminal article by the Chicago economist Milton Friedman in *The New York Times* in 1970, where he said,

> there is one and only one social responsibility of business – to use its resources and engage in activities designed to increase its profits, so long as it stays within the rules of the game, both those embodied in law and those embodied in ethical custom.[9]

Corporations do not have responsibilities, Friedman said, only executives do – and their responsibility as agents of their owners is to maximise shareholder returns. In any event "ethical custom", a somewhat throw-away term, never stood much chance in a straight fight with profit-maximisation.

The principle of the common good challenges Smith's utilitarian theory of rational self-interest most radically at the level not of "rationality" or "interest" but at the level of "self". Smith was a leading member of the Scottish Enlightenment, a philosophical school that helped to give birth to the modern notion of the "self" as an autonomous unit of consciousness, the self-defining individual who stands clear of any entanglements with others except in so far as they can do him some advantage. This self knows of its own existence not because it is loved and can love, i.e. in relationship, but because it can think rationally, i.e. enclosed in its own mental space, a form of Descartes' *cogito ergo sum*. This idea of the self as an unencumbered individual became the dominant idea of modern secular liberal democracy, an individualism that the culture takes for granted as normal, indeed normative. And when such an individual engages in finance or trade or economics, he is pleased to note that social obligations are not part of his responsibility, and he becomes, of course, the autonomous rational creature, *Homo economicus.*

So central to liberal individualism is this idea of the individual self, some have seen it as a threat to the very idea of the common good. To the highly influential American moral philosopher John Rawls, for instance, the individual has to make up his own mind about what is good, which may be in conflict with other ideas. There can be no consensus, no "common" agreement about what constitutes human flourishing because modern societies are pluralistic in character and draw their moral inspiration from diverse and sometimes contradictory sources. Thus the highest and only essential contemporary virtue is tolerance of difference, which translates into the prohibition of discrimination and the refusal to promote any one version of morality – of what is good – as preferable to any others.

Against Rawls and the utilitarian philosophy of Jeremy Bentham, Jesse Norman argues in his biography of Edmund Burke that liberal individualism "mistakes the true order of priority between the individual and society."[10] For Burke (himself an Enlightenment figure though an opponent of some of its protagonists such as Rousseau):

> a deeper mistake is seeing people as mere individual atoms. In effect it is a denial of their collective identities as participants in a social contract or between the generations: a denial of the covenantal nature of society itself. It seeks to assert the primacy of the individual will, and sees all social constraint as fetters to be thrown off. Liberty becomes license: the absence of impediments to the will. The danger then is that liberal individualism makes people profoundly selfish; that they slip from an enlightened to an unenlightened self-interest.[11]

This "covenantal nature of society" is close to the concept of the common good, one of many respects in which Burke's philosophy overlaps with Catholic Social Teaching. (Burke was an Irish Protestant son of an Irish Protestant father, though his mother and his wife were Catholics and he was frequently accused of being a secret one himself, even of being a Jesuit.)

are there universal moral truths?

Catholic Social Teaching and its advocacy of the common good can expect to make little progress in modern secular culture unless it can negotiate a way round Rawls' objection concerning moral consensus. How does it do so? Its critique of individualism is almost identical to that of Burke. But it can also embrace some of what Rawls is saying, by incorporating tolerance of diversity as an essential component of the common good while at the same time claiming to find a common set of values in all moral systems. Contemporary Roman Catholic doctrine does precisely this, which is a radical shift from previous attitudes.

The *Declaration on Religious Liberty* issued by the Second Vatican Council in 1965 declared:

> It is imperative that the right of all citizens and religious communities to religious freedom should be recognized and made effective in practice. Government is to see to it that equality of citizens before the law, which is itself an element of the common good, is never violated, whether openly or covertly, for religious reasons. Nor is there to be discrimination among citizens.[12]

It finds a common moral basis, transcending specific religious differences, in the "sense of the dignity of the human person which has been impressing itself more and more deeply on the consciousness of contemporary man." This reference to a universal moral consensus about human dignity is not so different from Rawls' insistence that there is a universal and rational basis for "fairness" on which principles of justice may be based. The demand that individuals "should act on their own judgment, enjoying and making use of a responsible freedom, not driven by coercion but motivated by a sense of duty" is declared in this crucial Vatican document to be "greatly in accord with truth and justice." Many have seen this as a concession to, or even the belated adoption of, the essential Enlightenment view of the freedom of the self, though with more emphasis on duties than on rights.

The principle of the common good is easier to describe than to define. In the fourth of his 2009 BBC Reith Lectures, the Harvard philosopher Michael Sandel, who is by background Jewish, offered no definition but argued for a new form of politics. "Unlike market-driven politics, a politics of the common good invites us to think of ourselves less as consumers, and more as citizens," he said.[13]

> Here's why this matters. Market-mimicking governance takes people's preferences as given and fixed. But when we deliberate as citizens, when we engage in democratic argument, the whole point of the activity is critically to reflect on our preferences, to question them, to challenge them, to enlarge them, to improve them.

Catholic Social Teaching does offer a definition of the common good, given in the document *Gaudium et Spes* of Vatican II as "the sum total of social conditions which allow people, either as groups or as individuals, to reach their fulfilment more fully and more easily." Other documents within this tradition[14] describe "fulfilment" as "integral human development": 'integral' meaning relating to the whole person in every aspect, which includes educational, emotional, physical, cultural, psychological, and spiritual factors but acting together rather than in isolation; 'human', embracing all that the word means, especially human dignity but also in mutual relationships that are beneficial and fruitful; and 'development' meaning growth in health and well-being and the realisation of all that a person has been given in his or her talents and capacities, or "capabilities". It has been described as "becoming whom one is meant to be" (which does however raise the theological question *meant by whom?*).

The philosopher Amartya Sen, whose background and sympathies are in Hinduism, and the Jewish philosopher Martha Nussbaum, have together expanded and enumerated the concept of "capability" that is generally consistent with Catholic Social Teaching on integral human development, leaving it free of the need for theological – if not cultural – underpinning.[15] Hence the 'meant by whom?' question does not always have to be answered theistically. Capability refers to the realisation of the potential present in the actual.

Again, the reference to spiritual development in the list of things covered by the phrase "integral human development" is not necessarily confined to religious observance, but should certainly include meditation and "mindfulness" practices, whether their basis is in theological or psychological ideas and beliefs, or both.

the common good illustrated

It can be helpful to illuminate the concept by using concrete examples. Take Laura and Emma, hypothetical teenage school friends. As well as progressing in their general education and well-being, Laura loves playing hockey while Emma is learning the violin. Emma likes watching Laura play, while Laura likes listening to Emma practise. They both want to be good at what they do, and they both want each other to be good at what they do too. Their gradual progress towards excellence in each field is not only satisfying and pleasurable to both of them, but is of real benefit to both of them, to their "integral human development". It forms their character.

They share, therefore, a "good" – their progress towards excellence in their particular skill – even though it is in different fields. We can call that a shared good, or a common good. The idea can readily be extended to the whole class, the whole school or college, and the whole community outside. Indeed the very existence of a school in which Laura and Emma can progress in their different ways is an expression of an attitude on the part of the community – and more than an attitude, a commitment – to the integral human development, by the full realisation of their capabilities, of all the children in that community. It represents also a political decision by the community, that that is the sort of society they want to live in, just as Laura wants to live in a society where Emma's talents are developed, and Emma wants to live in a society where Laura's talents are developed.

It is a product of the emphasis on the individual self in modern Western culture that choices such as these are not understood according to a calculus of the common good, but in terms of a polarised choice between selfishness and altruism. They are construed as zero-sum, that is to say the more selfish one is, the less altruistic, and vice versa. Laura's interest in Emma's progress is seen as unselfish and no doubt praiseworthy for that reason (unless one is Ayn Rand).

There is much cultural baggage attached to both these ends of the spectrum. While selfishness is less admirable, it is also seen as a basic human characteristic, maybe the most basic of all. There is a residual trace here of a Protestant ethic which sees human nature as fundamentally corrupt, or "totally depraved" as some Reformers put it. So is it natural for a human being to be selfish, more natural than being unselfish? Human nature may be fashioned from warped timber, but Thomas Hobbes' description in his *Leviathan* of everyone being perpetually engaged in a "war of every man against his neighbour" is more the exception than the rule. Nevertheless, if selfishness has to prevail because it defines human nature, much ingenuity has gone into trying to harness it for better purposes, such as providing a public benefit.

The early Enlightenment Anglo-Dutch writer Bernard Mandeville described it as the trick of turning "private vices" into "public virtues". This is the beauty of Adam Smith's proposition concerning the effect of an "invisible hand". Modern mainstream economics has taken to heart the notion that, though an individual may be operating in pursuit of self-interest in a free market economy, social benefits will arrive unbidden. Thus has what might otherwise have been seen as a human flaw been turned to good use. This kind of judgement stands at the heart of virtually all defences of free market economics on moral grounds: that it has the alchemy to turn bad into good, dross into gold. But it is rooted in an anthropology (and theology) of a corrupt human nature that is at least open to debate. It is characteristic of Catholic Social Teaching to be more optimistic than that.

The principle of the common good makes this assumed polarisation between selfish and altruistic choices redundant. Emma does not have to choose her own interests over and against Laura's, because she benefits from Laura's growth and development. And Laura reciprocates, to Emma's benefit. But they can also pursue their own good, for the benefit of themselves, of each other and of the wider whole. They participate and advance in a common good they share.

So well established is the idea that individuals are basically selfish and reluctant to contribute to the good of others, some people find this notion of a shared common good hard to accept. They fail to realise that the concept of the free individual self is a social construct of relatively recent origin, and that the identity of the self has no content until it is forged in relationships during the growth of the child. However much they may eventually emerge as individuals, human beings start life as social animals who must depend on others long before they can depend on themselves, and they are shaped by others long before they can take charge of their own destiny. Indeed, they can only learn how to do this from others. It is parents and teachers who show children how to stand on their own feet.

big society and civic virtue

The notion of a common good applies *par excellence* to families, through the mutual support that loving partners, married or otherwise, supply to each other for the benefit of both, and of any children they may have. Nobody sees that as altruism or measures each partner's share according to some index of selfishness: the principle of the common good is the natural and logical ethic of family life. It is, therefore, very familiar, and constantly being renewed.

There are other institutions in British society where the natural ethic is the common good principle. As well as the state school system already mentioned, the National Health Service is one obvious case. Both within the NHS and in the democratic and financial support the whole community gives to it, the NHS represents the principle that the healthcare interests of everyone are the responsibility of everyone. Few would regard paying tax to support the NHS as altruism or those who use the NHS as being selfish: it is a civic responsibility for a shared benefit – for the common good.

There is a theoretical difference between the idea of 'a' common good and 'the' common good, the first being more specific to a particular community, such as a school, town or region; the latter, which refers to the universal common good, having no limits. The difference comes where 'a' common good – promotion of the integral human development of Laura and Emma, to use our example – stands in the way of 'the' wider common good, for instance if their school could only succeed in what they do by denying facilities to other schools in the neighbourhood. In that case, a particular good stands in the way of the general common good, and has to be seen as not so good after all. So every particular good, to be genuinely good, has to be compatible with the furtherance of the universal good rather than get in its way. In most instances they neatly combine to reinforce each other. Emma's progress as a violinist enriches her, enriches her friends and family, enriches her school and the whole community: it enriches the whole of humanity.

Those who experience a 'divided' life as they pass between their place of work and the rest of their everyday lives are in fact passing between these two modes of moral consciousness – the 'everyday' social self where the culture and ethos of the common good is taken for granted as normative, and the 'workplace' where the culture of neoliberal individualism and ethos of self-interest is imposed by the exigencies of the job. There are signs that such individuals increasingly try to resolve the conflict by taking the values of the workplace into their home and social life – what has been called the 'marketisation' of the culture. It can mean the transfer of faith in an invisible hand – served by the rational pursuit of individual self-interest – from the economic sphere into non-economic affairs, including human relationships. The consequences are invariably unhappy, because it is based on a misreading of human nature. Catholic Social Teaching sets itself the opposite task: to close the gap the other way, so that the habits and customs of the service of the common good – the basic moral virtues – are also applied in the world of work.

But this also means reconfiguring certain core attributes of modern Britain, such as the revival of civil society – the project David Cameron has labelled the Big Society – because that is where the essential civic virtues such as a sense of duty, or reliability and trustworthiness, reside and are nurtured.

chapter 2 – references

1   Gillian Tett, *Fool's Gold: How Unrestrained Greed Corrupted a Dream, Shattered Global Markets and Unleashed a Catastrophe* (Abacus, 2010), p. 252.

2   bid. p. 253.

3   Anatole Kaletsky, *Capitalism 4.0: The Birth of a New Economy* (Bloomsbury, 2011, and Kindle), Chapter 11: 'There Is No Can Opener'.

4   Dominic Barton, Keynote address www.blueprintforbusiness.org/content/–download/31166/221759/file/dominic-barton-address.pdf (2012).

5   *Pretty Woman* (Touchstone Pictures, 1990).

6   *Vocation of a Business Leader: a Reflection* Pontifical Council for Justice and Peace (2012); www.hightail.com/download/M3BrT0NUY1NGR0VFSzhUQw

7   Mark Carney, *Inclusive Capitalism: Creating a sense of the Systemic* www.bankofengland.co.uk/publications/Pages/speeches/default.aspx (2014).

8   Adam Smith, *The Wealth of Nations* (1776).

9   Milton Friedman, 'The Social Responsibility of Business is to Increase its Profit' *New York Times Magazine* 13 September 1970.

10 Jesse Norman, *Edmund Burke: The Visionary Who Invented Modern Politics* (William Collins, 2013, and Kindle): Chapter 9: 'The Rise of Liberal Individualism'.

11 Ibid. p. Chapter 7, 'The Social Self'.

12 Second Vatican Council *Declaration on Religious Freedom* 1965; para. 6.

13 Michael Sandel, *A New Politics of the Common Good* http://downloads.bbc.co.uk/rmhttp/–radio4/transcripts/20090630_reith_anewpolitics.rtf (2009).

13 The encyclicals *Populorum Progressio* (1967) and *Caritas in Veritate* (2009) in particular.

14 Amartya Sen, *Commodities and Capabilities* (Oxford University Press, 1985).

loving the little platoon

the importance of being trusted

The proposition to be examined in this chapter is that Catholic Social Teaching can help to supply the tools to explain why the 2008 financial crash happened, and can therefore help to answer the important question – how do we prevent such a thing happening again? A key word turns out to be 'trust' – why it is necessary, why it declined, why neoliberal economists (and businesses run on those principles) thought they could do without it (or at least with only a minimum of it) and why, in the end, they couldn't.

An absence of trust signals an indifference to virtue, for who can trust a person whose ethical character is doubtful? This focuses attention back onto the central claim of neoliberal economics, that it is a system that can function – as does a science like physics – without the need for any moral underpinning except the maximisation of personal freedom. It utterly rejects, for instance, the concept of social justice – that some economic outcomes are morally better, more just, than others. Thus Friedrich von Hayek, one of the foremost protagonists of neoliberalism, piled up the epithets against social justice in his seminal 1976 work *Law, Legislation and Liberty*. He called it a "particularly dangerous superstition", a "mirage", a "will-o-the-wisp", an "empty formula" that meant "nothing at all", and "a quasi-religious belief with no content whatsoever."[1]

Others are more positive. The Labour peer and founder of the Blue Labour movement, Lord (Maurice) Glasman, who is Jewish, has said of it, "there is no more reasonable tradition from which to begin an analysis of the causes of the crisis of capitalism and no more fertile terrain out of which to begin to fashion a politics of the common good than Catholic Social Thought."[2] The Archbishop of Canterbury, Justin Welby, called it "one of the greatest treasures that the churches globally have to offer."[3]

why Catholic, why social?

What gives Catholic Social Teaching a claim to be heard? Economists and philosophers start from first principles, and so do Catholic theologians: in their case, that God created the world and everything in it, including humanity. They then look for what might be termed second principles: how to organise the world to best serve the interests of that humanity. They have developed a series of concepts and ideas which are faithful to their first principle. These do not constitute a blueprint, but are more a set of criteria that have to be applied in practice. Others who may not start from that same first principle, may nevertheless see in those second principles some fundamental truths that reflect an accurate reading of human nature and of how human societies function.

This teaching, while remaining faithful to its own first principle, takes on board knowledge that appears to be valid from every available source: biblical texts and the insights of other religions, ancient Greek philosophy and other philosophical systems, history, sociology, law, psychology, anthropology, economics; indeed all the human sciences. It is a synthesis, and the process of synthesising takes place against an empirical background of lived experience – what works and what doesn't. But it is also systematic, in that its ideas together form a more or less coherent description of human life and human society, what can go wrong with them and how to make them better. And it is always and everywhere a work in progress, rather than a finished and final statement.

Virtually all ethical systems, religious and secular, have as their core moral value a Golden Rule, often summarised as "do as you would be done by". In the version that comes from the Judaeo-Christian ethical tradition this is expressed in the formula "love your neighbour as yourself." At the foundations of Catholic Social Teaching are two principles related to this, the common good and human dignity. They stand together jointly and equally – with a warning neither to separate them nor to let one take precedence over the other.

The key documents of this tradition, known as the social encyclicals, have elaborated these principles and explored how they might apply to contemporary circumstances. The first, *Rerum Novarum,* was published in 1891 and addressed the plight of workers caught up in 19th century industrialisation and urbanisation. The most recent document, *Caritas in Veritate*, was directed at the causes of the 2008 economic and financial crisis.

The common good and human dignity lead directly to a pair of concepts which need to be observed in any social, political or economic system if it is to be stable and sustainable: solidarity and subsidiarity. Solidarity makes the observation that human beings are social beings, connected and dependent on one another, and asserts that, therefore, all members of society have obligations to one another. "All are responsible for all," as one encyclical expresses it.[4] This applies across the whole range of human activities. There is no domain where solidarity does not operate. Solidarity expresses a truth about human nature, a basic tribal instinct. Hence any economic theory that also claims to be based on truths about human nature ought to be compatible with it. That does raise serious questions about the neoliberal insistence on competition as a basic law of economic life, which has sometimes taken elements from Darwinism in order to claim that 'survival of the fittest' – which Darwin never actually preached – necessitates a state of perpetual rivalry for scarce resources. Though competition is part of nature, so is co-operation. It is solidarity which rescues human life from being what Thomas Hobbes described as "life in an unregulated state of nature", the aforementioned "war of all against all" – that is to say "solitary, poor, nasty, brutish, and short".[5]

But solidarity, left to itself, can exert a pressure towards collectivism – the notion that mutual responsibility can only satisfactorily be organised by joint action, for instance by the state on behalf of the community. It has a centralising, and therefore disempowering, tendency.

Subsidiarity is an equal and countervailing force to solidarity, pushing against centralisation and collectivism. It has an empowering effect. It is also based on a truth about human nature in human society: that individuals, small units, families, local societies, have a natural inclination towards self-determination and therefore to a degree of self-government.

As Catholic Social Teaching expresses it, this principle of social organisation is so important that to obstruct it is morally wrong. It is as relevant to the organisation of society as a whole as it is to any sub-division within it, including the institutions we call limited companies or business corporations. And as in the case of solidarity, if it is part of human nature, economic systems which also claim to be based on human nature cannot ignore it.

Burke's "public affections"

Edmund Burke made a famous reference to this idea which Catholic Social Teaching calls subsidiarity. "To be attached to the subdivision," he said, "to love the little platoon we belong to in society, is the first principle (the germ as it were) of public affections. It is the first link in the series by which we proceed towards a love to our country, and to mankind."[6]

Jesse Norman, in his commentary on this passage, points out its key significance to Burke's political philosophy of a theory of civil society, an identical point to that made by Catholic Social Teaching. "Institutions trap and store knowledge," he writes. "Composed of a myriad private interactions, traditions and practices as it is, the social order becomes a repository of shared knowledge and inherited wisdom."[7] Then, as Catholic Social Teaching does, he notes the relevance of this to economics:

> Among those institutions is that of the market… just as [Adam] Smith embeds the idea of a market in a broader moral context of human sympathy in his *Theory*

of Moral Sentiments, so Burke sees markets and other institutions as operating within, drawing from and contributing to a broader moral community. Neither is, in the modern sense, an out-an-out free trader

– meaning that neither of them would divorce the operation of markets from the moral standards operating in civil society, as neoliberalism is wont to do.

Catholic Social Teaching sees subsidiarity and solidarity as necessarily harnessed together, as each has a tendency which by itself would be destructive of the common good and human dignity. *Caritas in Veritate* puts it thus:

> The principle of subsidiarity must remain closely linked to the principle of solidarity and vice versa, since the former without the latter gives way to social privatism, while the latter without the former gives way to paternalist social assistance that is demeaning to those in need.[8]

There is a tension between them and a balance to be struck, and where that balance falls is a matter for negotiation between different interests.

Subsidiarity is stated in Catholic Social Teaching as the principle that

> a community of a higher order should not interfere in the internal life of a community of a lower order, depriving the latter of its functions, but rather should support it in case of need and help to co-ordinate its activity with the activities of the rest of society, always with a view to the common good.[9]

By higher order is generally meant the state, though it could equally apply to the internal structure of any organisation, such as central management in a business.

This is different from the superficially similar principle of devolution, which implies that power may rightfully belong to a central authority which may nevertheless find it convenient to delegate it to a local one. Subsidiarity sees things the other way round – central authority should not usurp the rightful powers of a local authority. The principle does implicitly recognise, however, that there are certain functions proper to a central authority, though always as a service to the lower ones. There are clearly circumstances permitted by subsidiarity where even the state may want to pool its sovereignty with other states, thus passing authority up the chain rather than down it. Defence and the environment would be two such examples.

This also has implications at the other end of the scale. Subsidiarity upholds the integrity and autonomy of family life, and the rights of parents. It insists that the authority of parents over their children, for instance, does not result from the state delegating its authority to parents but arises naturally from the status of parenthood itself.

civil society's essential purpose

Catholic Social Teaching explains how the neglect of civil society can undermine economic theory and practice. Civil society is by no means limited to what is sometimes called "the voluntary sector". It includes families, churches, clubs and similar voluntary bodies, social enterprises, Non-Government Organisations (NGOs), charities, political parties and trades unions, local campaigning groups, even sporting associations and bodies promoting recreational activities. They naturally mediate and moderate the sometimes deleterious effects of State policies or market forces on individuals, by standing between the individual, and the State or market – the so-called public or private sectors – in order to achieve collectively some shared objective that the whole community, or some section of the community, desires to see fulfilled. Such objectives range from shared worship in a church, chapel, temple or mosque, to the game of football or rugby and the study of local history or archaeology. Often the aim is the relief of hardship caused by poverty and homelessness. Their primary objective is not to make a profit nor to comply with the law, though they need to raise money to operate and the State may regulate some aspect of their activity in the name of the common good. In so far as they share a common aim it can be described as the "integral human development" of some section of the population or all of it. The institutions of civil society have often come into existence from the desire of people to meet their social or developmental needs without turning to government or commercial solutions.

The variety of forms within civil society has many blurred boundaries with public or commercial institutions. Bodies like the Church of England (by law established), the BBC (similarly), or even universities (which exist under Royal Charter), though manifestly part of civil society, are not totally outside the public or private sectors. Sometimes such judgements depend on their culture and behaviour, and their degree of independence from state or market. The goal of transferring bodies from the public sector into the domain of civil society has been a feature of public policy for some years, examples ranging from foundation hospital trusts detached from central NHS administration, to free schools and academies outside local authority control. In every case the intention is to achieve local accountability – in other words to comply with the defining principle of civil society, subsidiarity. Paradoxically, some of these reforms have in practice increased central state control rather than loosening it.

It is significant that under Catholic Social Teaching this reform is judged not just as expedient but as morally desirable. But it is not just a case of "less state, more civil society," a common but crude interpretation of what David Cameron's Big Society project was about. It is the complex search for the right balance between the two, recognising that the State also has responsibility for promoting the common good and can do so in ways not open to civil society by itself – not least because civil society, rich in human resources, tends to be poor in financial resources.

Thus, the voluntary sector had as a matter of public policy been favoured by successive governments for the delivery of a variety of social services, supported by local or central government funding. But the withdrawal of a large part of that funding as a result of severe cuts to local government budgets – decreed by Westminster – has undermined the work of many of those civil society agencies. It was obviously not healthy for so much of civil society to become dependent on government subsidy, not least because 'he who pays the piper calls the tune' but also because when paying the piper stops, the tune stops too. So the relationship between the state and civil society needs renegotiation under the twin prescriptions of Catholic Social Teaching, solidarity and subsidiarity. Far from being none of the State's business, the maintenance of a healthy civil society is an essential aim of modern government.

All this activity provides an essential training in civic virtue, something neither market forces nor state-made law can supply by themselves. Alexis de Tocqueville described what happens when intermediate institutions, the very stuff of civil society, disappear:

> It is especially dangerous to enslave men in the minor details of life. For my own part, I should be inclined to think freedom less necessary in great things than in little ones, if it were possible to be secure of the one without possessing the other… Subjection in minor affairs breaks out every day and is felt by the whole community indiscriminately. It does not drive men to resistance, but it crosses them at every turn, till they are led to surrender the exercise of their own will.[10]

Yet these literally demoralised people are the same people, as executives, managers and employees, who have to make the economy work. If they do not learn virtue through the activities of civil society they cannot bring it with them to work. Civil society is the primary school of virtue and the primary host, therefore, of what is called social capital, defined as "the network of relationships of trust, dependability, and respect for rules, all of which are indispensable for any form of civil coexistence."[11] If trust is a necessary ingredient in any economic system and for the success of any business venture, then the nurturing of it through the healthy functioning of civil society is essential.

> Man is a social animal; people naturally imitate each other; they co-operate and compete; and they established practices, habits, rules and codes of behaviour which make this cooperation and competition possible. Individually, good habits become internalised into virtues; collectively, they create institutions, and the result is what we would now call social capital or trust.[12]

Catholic Social Teaching identifies several clear threats to the common good arising from the way free markets operate when they are exclusively pursuing short-term profit. The 2008 crisis brought them to the fore and allowed them to be examined critically in a way that had not been possible before. It drew attention, for instance, to the way economic pressures distort and shrink civil society, which becomes squeezed between the two pincers of the market and the state. As *Caritas in Veritate* declares, "the exclusively binary model of market-plus-State is corrosive of society."

Instead of this binary model, Catholic Social Teaching proposes a triangle of forces: state, market and civil society. In fact, civil society comes first. A state's boundaries may move, transferring a city or town from one jurisdiction to another while its life continues; economic systems, likewise, may come and go. But the *polis* must continue. If civil society is the source of something essential to the functioning of the economy, such as the social capital present in networks of people who trust each other, then the diminishment of civil society necessarily means the decline of trust.

In the inner detailed working of the financial crisis which developed in the course of 2007-08, there is no trace of civil society having any influence, but plenty of it itself being influenced negatively. Networks of trust, which are the hallmark of civil society, would have enabled financial institutions to assure themselves that the business they were doing was sound, because they knew the people they were dealing with were honest and reliable. But the bank managers – the local custodians of social capital – had all been made redundant. Their many civic virtues were deemed old-fashioned and inefficient. Neoliberal economists felt they had removed the need for trust, both in principle – because untrustworthy operators would be eliminated by the creative destruction process – and more practically, by the use of devices which allowed the risks of untrustworthy behaviour to be absorbed, mainly through insurance and what was called "securitization". Because neoliberalism thinks of itself as a closed and self-sufficient system not in need of moral input from outside itself, the elimination of trust was a breakthrough. It also meant that the vice or virtue of a particular operator was neither here nor there. If he was a bad apple those he had affected could claim on their insurance.

Under securitization, individual financial assets such as mortgages are pooled with other assets, then repackaged and sold to third parties. This lessens the risk to an investor that an individual mortgage in which he had a share might be subject to default. Thus it became profitable to induce poor people to borrow money at attractively low "introductory" repayment rates, known as "teaser" rates, which they could afford, even though they would have failed any measure of trust. And it became profitable to secure such loans on poor quality property, again because the assumption was that house prices would always rise and never fall. So even if a default in making repayments resulted in repossession and eviction of the family concerned, as it often did when the teaser rates expired and more normal interest rates kicked in, the mortgage holder would always get his money back.

This property market in sub-prime mortgages did not need anyone to trust anyone. They could all be utter scoundrels and the system would still work. And it also became profitable – became, in fact, the driving force behind the whole phenomenon – to trade these securitized assets between finance houses, with each transaction earning a fee. As Gillian Tett described in her book *Fool's Gold*, they couldn't get enough of them. The price at which these assets were bought and sold bore no relation to any actual value in the real world. They were worth simply what someone else was prepared to pay for them. These were classic conditions for a bubble, a state of mutually reinforcing market euphoria described by Alan Greenspan as "irrational exuberance". History suggests that the one certain thing about euphoria is that sooner or later it will be replaced by its opposite, panic – what one economist called "euphoria with a minus sign".

And then the American housing market did what everybody concerned had assumed was impossible. It turned down, and house prices started to fall. This was the first snowball to roll, at the top of the impending neoliberal avalanche. The whole toxic system would never have existed had trust remained one of its core values – had people been asking whether what was happening was honest, whether those engaged in it had any integrity, and whether the assets being traded so exuberantly had any real value, or indeed whether anyone knew whether they did or not.

markets, morals and trust

Does a neoliberal economic system consume trust until it is exhausted, instead of contributing to the maintenance of trust? There are free market economists who maintained, at least up until 2008, that markets automatically generated the trust they needed – that trust was necessary to profitability and hence there was a market advantage to be gained by behaving in a trustworthy manner.

In an essay published in 2001, Professor Norman Barry, Professor of Social and Political Theory at Buckingham University, defended the neoliberal system from the charge that capitalism has no ethical autonomy or integrity and that therefore this deficiency must be corrected from outside the market system.[13] The representative spokesman for this attack is Wilhelm Röpke, one of the founding fathers of German *ordoliberalism*, who declared:

> The market, competition and the play of supply and demand do not create ethical reserves; they presuppose and consume them. These reserves must come from outside the market... Self-discipline, a sense of justice, honesty, fairness, chivalry, moderation, respect for human rights, firm ethical norms – all of these are things which people must possess before they go to market and compete with each other.[14]

Many scholars have noted the similarity between Röpke's economic theory, which was the foundation of the German social market economy, and Catholic Social Teaching. Certainly he relied on Catholic politicians like Konrad Adenauer for its implementation. And his statement about markets consuming rather than generating ethical reserves – running down social capital – are at the heart of the critique Catholic Social Teaching makes of neoliberalism. To this Professor Barry replied:

> The market system is morally self-sufficient and it develops its own codes of conduct... Business morality develops spontaneously through the development of those constraints on immediate gratification which the market system undoubtedly requires... Given the ubiquity of self-interest it can be shown that these conventions produce the optimal supply of virtue, that is, just enough to maintain the market.[15]

Barry argues that what enforces the minimum necessary set of standards among businessmen is the fact that they meet the same people again and again – business is a continuously repeated game – so that those who do not co-operate with the system are "bred out". Even if that is so, and to an extent it must be, that does not explain on what basis these individuals operating in the market place are judging one another, in order to identify those who are falling short and need to be shouldered out. But the biggest stick for enforcing good behaviour, he argued, is through being taken over by another company, "the ultimate disciplinary device".

> Business ethics writers often pointed to the successful non-Anglo-American economies that make little use of the method. Apparently they survive largely through a developed form of trust... Of course, trust is part of the genetic code of capitalism. On the other hand, trust might have few moral features at all; it is just a way of reducing the transaction costs in a largely anonymous society.
>
> Still, even in the context of a minimalist business ethics, trust is often overrated.[16]

He goes on to say that though level of trust in the United States is reasonably high,

> this may not be true of business. The stockholders do not trust the managers – they think they are opportunists and rent seekers – and managers do not trust the shareholders… But America is still the most successful economy in the world, it is also the one which fulfils the highest moral standards.

On that matter at least, a sceptical history is still considering its verdict.

Barry does not explain why the takeover of one corporation by another should necessarily correct faults in the trustworthiness of the company being taken over. Experience says that takeovers are just as likely to weaken the ethos of a business as to strengthen it. But more significantly, Barry identifies the key characteristic of what he calls successful non-Anglo American economies – in which he would include the German social market economic system – as being the way they "apparently" survive "largely through a developed form of trust." And they derive that trust, he observes, not from within the market system but from outside it. So trust is after all a key issue, just as Catholic Social Teaching said it was.

Since the 2008 crisis this has become less controversial than it was at the start of that decade. Thus, in his address referred to earlier, Mark Carney defined the importance of social capital precisely as did Pope Benedict in *Caritas in Veritate*, a fact not so surprising once it is taken into account that the Governor of the Bank of England is a practising Catholic. He told the conference:

> Social capital refers to the links, shared values and beliefs in a society which encourage individuals not only to take responsibility for themselves and their families but also to trust each other and work collaboratively to support each other… Nowhere is that need more acute than in financial markets; finance has to be trusted.[17]

Trust may occasionally be completely absent, as when doing business with a known fraudster. The more common experience is ignorance of whether someone is trustworthy or not, where prudence suggests treating individuals as untrustworthy even though they may not be. Of course, one may insure against being defrauded, one may employ an agency to check credit ratings, and one may routinely include a percentage lost through theft and fraud in one's profit and loss account as an extra expense which has to be passed on to every customer. These all add to the transaction cost, however, and therefore lead to lower efficiency – in extreme cases, even to a business going bankrupt.

In another essay in the same collection as Professor Barry's argument was published, Lord Brian Griffiths, former head of Margaret Thatcher's 10 Downing Street policy unit and also a former professor of economics, flatly rejected Barry's arguments. Asking whether a business corporation could function without moral standards, that is to say function amorally and in the absence of trust, he said:[18]

> The single objective of such a corporation would be the maximisation of profit. The corporation would operate within the law, but would be unconcerned with moral principles. It would question whether policy or action was legal or illegal but not whether it was right or wrong... A company with an amoral standard would be a cold, bleak and insecure environment in which to work... There would be a constant stream of disputes, conflicts and litigation. The commitment made by members of his team to the future of the company would be uncertain... One major consequence of an amoral culture is that the cost of doing business, what economists call 'transactions costs,' would be that much greater, and the firm will soon find itself at a competitive disadvantage.

ethics and inequality

In place of neoliberal economics, Catholic Social Teaching advocates a return to the ethical basis of classical economics that would have been fully familiar to Adam Smith and Edmund Burke. *Caritas in Veritate* declares:

> Insofar as they are instruments, the entire economy and finance, not just certain sectors, must be used in an ethical way so as to create suitable conditions for human development and for the development of peoples...the intention to do good must not be considered incompatible with the effective capacity to produce goods.

Where are these genuinely ethical foundations to be rediscovered? In civil society, of which subsidiarity is the fundamental principle. Subsidiarity, often regarded as one of the more right-wing or individualistic aspects of Catholic Social Teaching (certainly when compared with solidarity), therefore presents in this respect a strong case against neoliberal ideology.

Caritas in Veritate also identifies another factor which, beyond a certain degree, constitutes a threat to civil society as an indirect consequence of market forces left to run free without regard for the common good – that is to say, growing inequality. But it is not just the wealth of elites and oligarchs *per se* that the encyclical sees as a threat to the social order, but the undermining of social capital. Democracy rests on the consent of the governed. That consent requires at least a minimum of trust that the promise of mass prosperity will be fulfilled, while as Phillip Blond points out, the political economy is now heading in the opposite direction, concentrating prosperity more and more in the hands of a wealthy oligarchy. Catholic Social Teaching has in principle accepted social and economic inequality as acceptable unless it has these damaging side effects, though it has clearly reached a point beyond which it should not go. Yet, over the past 30 years, overall wage inequality in Britain has reached the point where the top fifth of earners now earn on average 14 times as much as the bottom fifth. The graph of inequality over that time scale follows a similar pattern to the graph of the decline of trust, strongly suggesting one is causing the other.

At the same conference as Mark Carney, Christine Lagarde of the IMF, also a Catholic, quoted Pope Francis, saying he

> recently put this in stark terms when he called increasing inequality the root of social evil. It is therefore not surprising that IMF research – which looked at 173 countries over the last 50 years – found that more unequal countries tend to have lower and less durable economic growth.[19]

A study by three British academics, entitled *Catholic Social Teaching and the Firm,* looked at the circumstances which led Lloyds Bank to mis-sell certain insurance products to customers. While noting the perverse effect resulting from the wrong sort of incentives and rewards for staff, they also observed:

> There is well-documented concern that those at the top of organisations which pay very high multiples (of the order of hundreds of times) of the pay of average workers, thereby lose the willingness of employees to co-operate. In other words if employees perceive that the senior management is there mainly to line their own nests, any sense that the organisation is pursuing a good purpose…will be difficult to maintain.[20]

This describes a fundamental breakdown in trust between employees and their senior managers resulting from extreme inequality in a firm's remuneration structure.

It is a principle of Catholic Social Teaching that property rights are not unlimited, and that ownership of wealth brings with it a "social mortgage", that is to say a claim of right against a property owner on behalf of someone who does not have enough support, through no fault of his own, to live a reasonably healthy life. Indeed the principle that everyone has a duty to safeguard human life, including his or her own life, has traditionally been understood as justifying someone stealing a loaf of bread, if that is the only way he can save himself from starvation. But the elimination of all inequality is not, nor has it ever been, an objective of Catholic Social Teaching. Its insistence has always been on everyone having enough, rather than everyone having the same. This is deduced from the principle in Catholic Social Teaching called the Universal Destination of Goods: regardless of how property and other economic rights are distributed (and these rights will change as the mode of production changes) the use of property has to be for the benefit of the common good.

This is less controversial than it looks, as states have always possessed the reserve power to take over land or other assets for the benefit of the community, and the power to tax property, wealth and income. It does mean, however, that the ownership of property is always conditional upon it being put to some socially useful purpose, which would exclude, for instance, land hoarding as a mean of speculative investment. Furthermore the Universal Destination of Goods provides a framework that can legitimise the capitalist enterprise. When someone with capital ("goods to spare") uses it to provide a productive capacity such as a factory, it can result in employment and decent pay for workers, commercial opportunities for suppliers, a supply of useful services or products for customers, a just return to shareholders and profits taxable by the government. That list of beneficiaries may not entirely be a "universal destination" but it is getting there.

In the latest document in the Catholic Social Teaching corpus, *Evangelii Gaudium*, issued in 2013, Pope Francis is scathing about the injustice and cruelty which follow from extreme inequality:

> Just as the commandment "Thou shalt not kill" sets a clear limit in order to safeguard the value of human life, today we also have to say "thou shalt not" to an economy of exclusion and inequality. Such an economy kills… Today everything comes under the laws of competition and the survival of the fittest, where the powerful feed upon the powerless. As a consequence, masses of people find themselves excluded and marginalized: without work, without possibilities, without any means of escape.

There are tendentious versions of Catholic Social Teaching which minimise or even belittle the role of the state, often in the name of subsidiarity. Pope Francis seems to have them in mind when he says, in the same document:

> It is the responsibility of the State to safeguard and promote the common good of society. Based on the principles of subsidiarity and solidarity, and fully committed to political dialogue and consensus building, it plays a fundamental role, one which cannot be delegated, in working for the integral development of all.

Nor does he give any comfort to those who argue that markets are and must be allowed to remain autonomous, beyond the writ of governments to intervene.

While the earnings of a minority are growing exponentially, so too is the gap separating the majority from the prosperity enjoyed by those happy few. This imbalance is the result of ideologies which defend the absolute autonomy of the marketplace and financial speculation. Consequently, they reject the right of States, charged with vigilance for the common good, to exercise any form of control.

There is a tendency, particularly on the American right, to suggest that Pope Francis is breaking with the consistent pro-business message of Pope John Paul II, most notably in his encyclical *Centesimus Annus*. But in 1999, in an apostolic exhortation addressed to Catholics in America, John Paul specifically addressed neoliberalism by name, saying it was "based on a purely economic conception of man," a system which:

> considers profit and the law of the market as its only parameters, to the detriment of the dignity of and the respect due to individuals and peoples. At times this system has become the ideological justification for certain attitudes and behaviour in the social and political spheres leading to the neglect of the weaker members of society.[21]

This is one of many examples of a consistent theme of Catholic Social Teaching's main documents, which since 1891 have repeatedly referred to "unbridled" or *laissez faire* capitalism as a threat to the poor. But the same documents invariably resist drawing the conclusion that Karl Marx drew – that capitalism generates its own equal and opposite force, the proletariat, with whom it becomes locked in revolutionary struggle and whose ultimate triumph is guaranteed. Marxism relies on ineluctable historical forces and has no use for what it regards as "bourgeois" morality, and therefore like neoliberalism believes it does not need social capital, such as trust, to function.

chapter 3 – references

1   Friedrich Hayek, *Law, Legislation and Liberty: A new statement of the liberal principles of justice and political economy* (Routledge Classics, 1973, and Kindle). Chapter 9: 'Social or Distributive justice: The Conquest of public imagination by 'social justice".

2   Lord (Maurice) Glasman, *The Crisis of Capitalism and the Politics of the Common Good* Margaret Beaufort Lecture (Cambridge, 2011).

3   Vatican Radio, March 2013.

4   Pope John Paul II, *Sollicitudo Rei Socialis* (1987).

5   Thomas Hobbes, *Leviathan* (1651).

6   Edmund Burke, *Reflections on the Revolution in France* (1790).

7   Jesse Norman, *Edmund Burke: The Visionary Who Invented Modern Politics* (William Collins, 2013, and Kindle): Chapter 7. 'The Social Self'

8   Pope Francis, *Caritas in Veritate,* para 58.

9   Pope John Paul II, *Centesimus Annus*, 1991, para. 48.

10   Alexis de Tocqueville, *Democracy in America* (1840).

11   *Caritas in Veritate* (2009), para. 32.

12   Jesse Norman, *ibid, 'The Social Self'.*

13   Norman Barry, 'Ethics, conventions and capitalism' in *Capitalism, Morality and Markets* (Institute of Economic Affairs, 2001), p. 57.

14   Wilhelm Röpke, *A Humane Economy* (London: Wolf. 1960 and Kindle) p. 125.

15   Norman Barry 'Ethics, conventions and capitalism', p. 58.

16   Ibid. p. 64.

17   Mark Carney, *Inclusive Capitalism: Creating a sense of the Systemic* (2014).

18   Brian Griffiths, 'The business corporation as a moral community' in *Capitalism, Morality and Markets* (Institute of Economic Affairs, 2001) p. 20.

19   Christine Lagarde, *Economic Inclusion and Financial Integrity* www.imf.org/external/np/speeches/2014/052714.htm (2014).

20   G Moore, R Beadle and A Rowlands, *Catholic Social Teaching and the Firm. Crowding in virtue: a MacIntyrean approach to business ethics* (American Catholic Philosophical Quarterly 2014).

21   Pope John Paul II, Apostolic Exhortation *Ecclesia in America* (1999), para. 56.

the 30 trillion dollar question

inserting morality into the economic argument

Social capital, trust and virtue are a cluster of related concepts that are very important to Catholic Social Teaching. Where do they come from? As well as biblical sources, a fundamental influence in this area of moral philosophy and theology has been exercised by classic Greek philosophers, notably Aristotle. His influence waned at the end of the classical period but was revived, indeed rediscovered, through the impact of Islamic philosophers in mediaeval Spain, who had kept the Aristotelian spirit alive along with many other areas of Greek learning such as mathematics and medicine.

In philosophy their impact was greatest on Christian thinkers like Thomas Aquinas. What Aristotle brought to the debate via Aquinas was the development of the concept of 'the good' as the realisation of human potential – of becoming what one was meant to be – and of 'virtue', behaving as one ought to behave if one was actually to advance 'the good' of oneself and others. By practising the virtues one strove after 'excellence', which was good in itself. It is fair to note that other philosophical schools are sceptical of such concepts. But in ordinary speech, both the idea of 'virtue' – in essence, a judgement of a person's moral character – and 'the good' are still familiar and well understood (as are their opposites).

The virtue of solidarity – essentially 'loving your neighbour as yourself' – is closely related in Catholic Social Teaching to the common good. It is described as the acceptance of the moral obligations that arise from fully recognising the interdependence of all human life:

> This then is not a feeling of vague compassion or shallow distress at the misfortunes of so many people, both near and far. On the contrary, it is a firm and persevering determination to commit oneself to the common good; that is to say to the good of all and of each individual, because we are all really responsible for all.[1]

Solidarity in this treatment is extremely political. It requires a commitment to the common good that is "based on the solid conviction that what is hindering full development is that desire for profit and that thirst for power already mentioned" – referring to an earlier passage where the encyclical speaks of "on the one hand, the all-consuming desire for profit, and on the other, the thirst for power, with the intention of imposing one's will upon others."

It goes on to invoke the powerful concept of "structures of sin" – internal structural frameworks and systems within institutions that cause injustice and oppression – which can only be overcome

> by a diametrically opposed attitude: a commitment to the good of one's neighbour with the readiness, in the Gospel sense, to 'lose oneself' for the sake of the other instead of exploiting him, and to 'serve him' instead of oppressing him for one's own advantage.

The value of the "structure of sin" concept is that it shows how a political or economic institution can act sinfully, without personal responsibility for that sin necessarily falling wholly on any one individual. What many commentators in the run-up to the 2008 crisis, including those quoted in Chapter 1, may have missed is the way financial institutions can give great leverage to small acts of individual self-interest, amplifying their harmful effects far beyond what the actor intended.

An important corollary of the principle of the common good is that persons and communities who are economic *actors* are also moral actors. Hence all economic choices, whether as consumers, business-leaders, bankers, or policy-makers, inescapably have a moral dimension – often far greater than an individual may have bargained for. Leverage, a term usually used by financiers to refer to the technique of lending and borrowing money on a scale far greater than the resources of the institution concerned, is clearly only one of the ways that the institution's influence can be amplified many times over. The concept of 'structures of sin' explains how, by analogy with 'leverage', a small mistake in the world of finance can do much harm to many people.

Unlike Marxism, Catholic Social Teaching does not reject wealth creation, or assume that "all property is theft" – though someone who has plenty of it has obligations to someone with none. It recognises that markets are invaluable in the efficient distribution of resources, which helps the common good to flourish. It accepts competition in the market place, as an aid to efficiency and to product development. It recognises profit as a necessary product of and incentive for business activity, and understands that such activity can be risky and hence that those who engage in it should be properly rewarded. Hence Catholic Social Teaching is in its very nature business-friendly. If it resists

Catholic Social Teaching is in its very nature business-friendly.

an unwavering emphasis on the short-term maximisation of shareholder value, it does so because of the consequential cost to humanity – the costs which businesses, run on such lines, often export to the wider community, costs which economists call "externalities". The burden of coping with those costs usually falls on those least able to bear them, which is a severe injustice.

The major externality the world is still contending with is the damage to the global economy resulting from the 2007-08 economic meltdown. The greater long-term externality is undoubtedly damage to the environment, including health costs. When the Chinese Government tried to measure this factor by producing what it called a "Green GDP" figure – broadly, industrial output minus environmental damage – the annual increase in Chinese GDP was almost wiped out. So the Green GDP approach was abandoned; the truth it revealed was too painful.[2]

The argument that short-termism also harms business profitability in the long term is a practical as well as a moral one. Catholic Social Teaching would also assert that profitability is both necessary and desirable, as a sign that the goods or services being produced are meeting a need in the community. But it warns against the "temptation of seeking only short-term profit, without regard for the long-term sustainability of the enterprise, its benefit to the real economy."[3] As the Chinese GDP example shows, profitability cannot be the only test. Catholic Social Teaching therefore repudiates, on both rational and moral grounds, Milton Friedman's edict that "the business of business is business."

structures of sin?

Catholic Social Teaching says that the type of financial capitalism that resulted in the 2008 crisis was damaging to the common good. But whether it was the individuals concerned who neglected the common good in a way that was subjectively immoral, or whether it was the case that their economic world-view or ideology told them it had no relevance to what they were doing and hence that they were not morally culpable, is a much-debated point to which the concept of 'structures of sin' is highly relevant.

The embrace of a neoliberal view of economics is intrinsically a moral rather than a purely technical decision. To categorise a particular decision as not an ethical decision itself requires an ethical decision. Therefore, to regard shareholders as the only people with a right to an interest in the way a company is run, for instance, disregarding employees, customers, suppliers, and the environment as having no legitimate stake, is itself an ethical decision.

There is a widespread assumption in business, which seems to be based more on prejudice than on evidence, that ethics comes at a cost; in other words that neoliberalism, in which ethics is discounted, is by far the most efficient system. This is both the challenge and the opportunity that Catholic Social Teaching offers to all engaged in economic activity or in theorising about it. More and more emerging national economies are using competitive markets as their dynamic force but find themselves apparently faced with an invidious choice between morality and efficiency, ethics versus economics. This poses a number of questions for them. Is this choice necessary, or can these apparent opposites be reconciled? Is the neglect of human, social and ethical issues in the operation of economic systems actually wasteful, and therefore inefficient? Is there a better anthropology, truer to human nature, than *Homo economicus*? Would an alignment of ethics and economics make not just for better ethics but better economics? And could the principles of Catholic Social Teaching proof newly emerging financial and economic systems against the grievous errors that led to 2008? That is the 30 trillion dollar question.

Catholic Social Teaching reinforces the view that support for the common good does in the long term help business in the creation of wealth – not purely in cash terms, but in the adding of extra value by producing goods and services that benefit humanity. The common good is part of the social glue that holds societies together and enables them to function. Business leaders know that a society that does not hold together and which therefore becomes dysfunctional will soon become an unfavourable environment in which to operate. And a functioning society which detects that a business operating within it is indifferent to its common good may rebel against that business. Regulators may force it to behave better, customers may shun it, NGOs may campaign against it, shareholders may demand a change of policy or personnel at the top. Ultimately it may go out of business, particularly if these social disapproval factors are allied to lower efficiency resulting from disregarding the common good.

There is also an anthropological reason why Catholic Social Teaching can claim to be pro-business. If it is right in its fundamental assumptions about human nature, then the most efficient system will be the one that harnesses that nature, goes with the grain of it, thereby maximising its potential. Economic systems which go against the grain of human nature will have to use some of their energy fighting human nature. They will therefore be wasteful. It is a truism that a business person who treats his employees as human beings gets a better result out of them.

Not just for better profitability, however, but because they have become aware of the need for a more human-friendly way of running a business, a growing number of business leaders are looking for ways of raising their game by transforming the ethos and culture of their enterprise.

chapter 4 – references

1   John Paul II, *Sollicitudo Rei Socialis* (1987), para. 38.

2   'Choking on Growth' *New York Times* 26 August 2007.

3   *Caritas in Veritate* (2009), para. 40.

redeeming the market

how to reform business culture

Catholic Social Teaching can offer a guide to employers on how to treat employees as human beings, as well as how to operate as good citizens. The key documents of the Catholic Social Teaching tradition are the so-called social encyclicals issued by a succession of Popes. Leo XIII published the first, *Rerum Novarum*, in 1891. Subsequent encyclicals, as far as 1991, have been welded into a whole in a document called the *Compendium of the Social Doctrine of the Church*, published in 2004, thus predating *Caritas in Veritate* from 2009.

Pope John Paul II's *Centesimus Annus* of 1991 discussed the world economic system in the aftermath of the collapse of the Soviet empire. It rejected communism and socialism, as had all previous documents in the series, and favoured a market-based economic model, while protesting at many of the injustices that kept poorer nations in a state of poverty. But it also contained many salient warnings of what could happen if economic systems did not heed the common good, though it did not foresee the degree of collapse nor the scale of the consequences. Those were addressed fully in the 2009 document.

It is a tradition that each document in the series either explicitly repeats the arguments advanced in previous documents or takes them as read, though the comparison of one document with another does reveal shifts in tone and emphasis. The document *Evangelii Gaudium* of Pope Francis is not an encyclical in the traditional sense but contains a long section on economics and the common good, and is therefore the latest addition to this collection. It is sharper in its tone than some of its predecessors.[1]

This sequencing of documents makes it clear that while the fundamentals of Catholic Social Teaching are, as the name implies, part of the Catholic Church's official doctrine, this is also a body of work in progress, changing as circumstances and the intellectual context change. For decades it was engaged in a simultaneous debate with capitalism and communism; since 1989 the latter has received much less attention.

These papal documents are usually assembled from various drafts contributed by international experts, including social scientists, economists and theologians. From that raw material a Pope selects those he approves of as being consistent with the tradition, adds his personal contribution, usually to address a particular situation or recent development, and weaves them into a whole. Sometimes there is considerable internal debate among the Pope's advisers, and sometimes outside groups try to lobby in order to influence the outcome. They tend not to succeed.

From within this tradition, and as a result of the academic discipline called Catholic Social Thought, a number of secondary documents have been produced which explore the implications of some of the major themes in more detail or in specific local contexts. Attention has already been paid to the project *Blueprint for a Better Business*, launched in 2012 by the Roman Catholic Archbishop of Westminster as a result of conversations with various prominent business leaders. They had expressed to him an interest in renewing the moral and philosophical basis on which modern business operated, an implicit recognition that the fashion for value-free neoliberalism was passing, having failed to predict or prevent the 2008 crisis. They agreed to see whether Catholic Social Teaching, especially its fundamental principle of the common good, could meet that need.

Blueprint for a Better Business was run by a steering group – of which the author of this essay was a member – before it became an independent charitable trust in the summer of 2014.[2] Its members are mostly from the business world and are committed to the application of Catholic Social Teaching in that world. In conversation with a number of unofficial partners the group designed what it called a "framework document". This was intended to offer managers and executives a set of practical criteria, in non-technical language, to enable them to ensure that decisions and policies were tailored to advancing the common good.

Their key insight was that every business needs a clear statement of its purpose – of what it is committed to, what it exists to do – which will enable all who engage in the business to focus on the common project and tell those who join the project what it is they are joining. It does not have to be visionary but it does have to be compelling, achievable and realistic. Such a statement creates loyalty on the part of employees, encourages joint effort at all levels, fosters a sense of vocation and enables those who work for the company in whatever capacity to feel proud that they are making a contribution to the wider good of society. This also wards off the possibility that the business will be seen to exist only to maximise short-term shareholder value. Such a business has its own common good, for which all take responsibility and where all share in the resulting progress and prosperity.

To this end they defined *Five Principles for a Purpose-Driven Business*, as an aid to business leaders who wish to think about what they do and how they do it. The *Principles* lead them through a series of topics that need to be addressed if a business is to be ethically well-grounded.

The first asserts that a good business is honest and fair with customers and suppliers, in that it seeks to build lasting relationships with customers and suppliers, deals honestly with customers providing good and safe products and services, treats suppliers fairly, pays promptly what it owes and expects its suppliers to do the same, and openly shares its knowledge to enable customers and suppliers to make better-informed choices.

The second declares that a good business is a good citizen, in that it considers each person affected by its decisions as if they were a member of each decision-maker's own community, seeks and provides access to opportunities for less privileged people, and makes a full and fair contribution to society by structuring its business and operations to promptly pay all taxes that are properly due.

The third states that good business

> has a purpose which delivers long-term sustainable performance, operates true to a purpose that serves society, respects the dignity of people and so generates a fair return for responsible investors, and enables and welcomes public scrutiny of the alignment between stated purpose and actual performance.

The fourth principle argues that a good business has to be a responsible and responsive employer, which treats everyone with dignity and provides fair pay for all, enables and welcomes constructive dialogue about its behaviour in keeping true to its purpose, fosters innovation, leadership and personal accountability, and protects and nurtures all who work for it to ensure people also learn, contribute and thrive.

Finally, a good business is a guardian for future generations, because it honours its duty to protect the natural world and conserve finite resources, contributes knowledge and experience to promote better regulation to the benefit of society as a whole rather than protecting self-interest, and invests in developing skills, knowledge and understanding in wider society to encourage informed citizenship.

principles of good business

Most documents in the area of Catholic Social Teaching and Thought are heavy with quotations and footnotes referring to other documents in the same tradition, showing the source of the ideas expressed and how they have been developed, and also demonstrating consistency with earlier documents. It was a deliberate choice of the designers of the "framework document" that, while staying faithfully within the parameters of Catholic Social Teaching, they would not offer quotations and footnotes nor refer specifically to source documents. The primary target for this framework is people in a business environment, who may possibly have MBAs but probably not a degree in moral theology. Thus to improve readability, the framework has to stand on its own merits.

This is equally true of the *Framework to Guide Decision Making*[3] to which the *Five Principles* are the introduction. The framework is necessary because the ethical basis of a business cannot be left as a vague philosophical abstraction or pious moral assertion – most businesses have experimented with such things in the past and have found that they do not relate to everyday business life and therefore make little difference. Such gestures do not change culture, and they do not encourage or reward virtue.

The Framework to Guide Decision Making translates and expands on the two key values at the heart of Catholic Social Teaching: human dignity and the common good. It explains the heading "Dignity and Value of People" as "Each person is a someone, not a something". It then urges persons in business to show respect for the dignity of each person and for the whole person; never use people merely as a means to achieving business objectives. Respecting the whole person, it says, includes thinking of people in all their various roles in relation to the business: as employees, customers, suppliers, investors, and citizens. Demonstrating respect means setting a purpose and seeking outcomes that enable each person to reach his or her full potential, not least being able to contribute fully to building relationships and communities both within the workplace and beyond. "Such purposes and such outcomes engender trust between people and between business and society."

It interprets the concept of the common good to mean, for businesses, "delivering value by serving society". Hence businesses should genuinely aim to promote the good of society as a whole through the provision of goods and services that benefit society; and never use stakeholders, and society as a whole, as a mere means to business success. "This gives meaning to the purpose of the business within society and demands innovation to achieve that purpose alongside a financial return."

It recognizes that it is society itself that determines the laws and regulations which permit business to operate. For instance, the public limited liability company is a creation of law, whose privileges, for instance the protection against personal bankruptcy given to shareholders, are conditional on responsible behaviour in return. Business must actively aim to reduce harm arising from its activities and produce "goods that are truly good and services that truly serve." This is a careful paraphrase of what many documents in the official Catholic Social Teaching tradition have said about the duties of those engaged in business.

It then moves on to discuss issues of behaviour and character, addressing each of them, implicitly, in terms of principles normally derived from Catholic Social Teaching. These are all ways, CST says, that businesses can seek to contribute to the common good. It urges business leaders to

> acknowledge and seek to measure the impact the business has on people, values, resources, and the environment. Accept responsibility for those impacts. Then take steps to develop people, nurture values, preserve and restore existing resources and create new ones where possible so that others may enjoy their benefits. Use your knowledge, influence and experience in collaboration with others for the benefit of all.[4]

The stewardship of people is a characteristic concern of Catholic Social Teaching, and has been from the beginning. It was this which marked the first encyclical in the sequence, *Rerum Novarum*, in 1891. Its name, literally 'New Things', referred to the condition of the new industrial working classes that were becoming a familiar feature of European and American cities – and of political debate – as the Industrial Revolution spread outwards from its British heartland, based on manufacturing and mass production. It wasn't so new, of course. The Catholic Church had a lot of catching up to do. *Rerum Novarum* was partly a sincere and sensitive response to the condition of the working class, which was in many cases appalling. But it was also triggered by alarm at the extent to which many workers were being attracted to Communism in protest at those conditions. The Church feared communism not just because of its atheism and anticlericalism but because it was a revolutionary threat to the status quo.

dignity of the worker

Rerum Novarum's insistence on the dignity of the worker, and on the rights that dignity brings with it, are still key ideas. Any critique of free market capitalism, where it has gone wrong and how it might reform, has to address this issue. The document in the Catholic Social Teaching tradition which dealt with it in detail was the encyclical *Laborem Exercens* of 1981.[5] Its historical significance is that it was written by a Polish Pope just when the Polish anti-communist trade union Solidarity was growing in strength. Not surprisingly, therefore, it sets out a Catholic view of workers' rights specifically to highlight deficiencies in the Marxist view of workers' rights (or the lack of them), which is what Solidarity was campaigning against. This was undoubtedly one of the ways that Pope John Paul II (formerly Karol Wojtyla, Archbishop of Cracow) helped to destabilise Polish Communism, thereby loosening the ideological bricks out of which the Berlin Wall – and all it stood for – was constructed.

In principle, the Communist State owns the labour of the working class as much as any slave master, and may punish those workers who refuse to do such work as the state tells them. There is no freedom to withhold labour or to bargain. Under a Marxist regime, the theory says, workers have already overcome the conflicts of interest between capital and labour, and live in a situation described as the dictatorship of the proletariat. In such a utopian condition workers have no need of rights vis-à-vis the state. They are the state. The collective has extinguished the individual.

In Catholic theory, the worker owns his own labour and may dispose of it freely. If he cannot get a fair price for it from an employer on his own, because he is at an extreme disadvantage due to the inequality of power between them, he may join with others to negotiate jointly. He may refuse to work – that is to say, strike – if he is not satisfied with the outcome.

Under *laissez faire*, on the other hand, it is the employer who goes to market to buy labour, and pays only as much as is necessary to get the amount he needs. He owns the means of production, which the labourer must have access to if he is to give his work any value. Ownership of the means of production is the essence of capitalism, for it is only by the expenditure of 'capital' that those means of production exist at all. This means he is entitled to benefit from the inequality between himself and the worker. Collective bargaining is a denial of free market forces. The individual has extinguished the collective.

Thus does capital win over labour. Beyond paying wages, such a capitalist has no responsibilities towards those he employs, unless the state imposes responsibilities on him. The labourer sells his labour as a commodity, to be bought and sold on the labour market: it is then no longer his, but his employer's. This 'alienation' of the worker from his labour, as if they were two separate entities, is not acceptable to Catholic Social Teaching but regarded as an injustice.

Laborem Exercens regards work ideally as creative, and sees 'man' (that is to say men and women[6]) as possessing an inalienable vocation (a calling) to work, and not simply to provide for himself and his dependents. Theologically – and this was controversial at the time – man's creativity is presented as an extension of God's creativity, man being made in God's image. This concept of co-creativity, of co-operating with the divine, elevates work to a high and noble status. The natural creativity of human beings should therefore be respected and esteemed, protected and nurtured.

This is at odds with an alternative strand in Christianity that treats work as a chore and the need to work as virtually a punishment, part of Original Sin. One consequence of this difference is that in the Catholic view of work, workers have a right to enjoy it. It fulfils their creativity. 'Job satisfaction' is natural, normal and necessary. But that also means that they have an innate desire to work, and they have a right to work. So being prevented from working is an unnatural state, harmful to the individual, a denial of human dignity.

In this perspective, people would not prefer to be idle. They would rather work than not. But there is also an obligation on the organiser of the work, usually an employer, to make it as creative as possible, so that the individual has as much control as possible over the work he does, and as much pride and satisfaction as possible at the end of it. This condition is not met if the work in question consists simply of one task repeated hundreds of times throughout the working day. It also means that work is part of integral human development. Work contributes to the good of the worker and hence to the common good. Far from work being undignified – or worse, something to be avoided if at all possible – the right to work is an inalienable consequence of human dignity.

Many of these insights happen to coincide with what industrial psychology has discovered about human motivation in the work place. Treating workers with respect, 'giving them a say', improves both productivity and industrial relations. But Catholic Social Teaching goes further, and says in principle labour takes precedence over capital because labour is human and capital merely material. It therefore asserts that the workforce is a major stakeholder in a business alongside its shareholders, and should therefore have a share in decision-making. Company structures that reflect Catholic Social Teaching, for example in Germany, routinely include representatives of the workforce on company boards. As a result employees understand their share of responsibility for the success of the company, and there is not the 'us and them' attitude of employees towards managers. This can be a crucial factor in wage bargaining, and in discouraging industrial action.

It also has implications for the way management manages change, which can be one of the most important, difficult and stressful aspects of the vocation of a business manager. To be able to engage directly and share decision-making with representatives of the workforce enables managers to find consensual solutions which are a fair balance between different interests. The arrangement symbolises the truth that wealth creation requires both labour and capital, and the task of management is to find the best relationship between them that serves both of them. This can mean painful choices, including limits on pay, job reductions, plant or branch closures, etc. and also restraint on executive pay and bonuses, but the best circumstances for handling those choices is when the interests of the stakeholders can be taken into account in the course of the decision-making process. The German experience is fairly clear that co-determination can actually increase the range of options

> The workforce is a major stakeholder in a business alongside its shareholders, and should therefore have a share in decision-making.

open to management to handle necessary change, while keeping the risk of industrial conflict to a minimum.

Lord Glasman, in his lecture in Cambridge quoted earlier, highlighted the emphasis that Catholic Social Teaching gives to work and labour. *Rerum Novarum*, he said, established the link

> between the Catholic theory of the person and the institutional arrangements organised around the idea that work is transformative of both nature and self. 'By your sweat shall ye live' is our fallen fate. The priority of the value of labour over capital is central to this thesis. In *Laborem Exercens* Pope John-Paul II wrote 'Man is a person, that is to say a subjective being capable of acting in a planned and rational way, capable of deciding about himself and with a tendency to self-realisation. As a person man is the subject of work… these act to realise his humanity, to fulfil a calling to be a person that is his by reason of his humanity… Labour is a primary efficient cause, while capital, the whole collection of means of production, remains a mere instrument or instrumental cause'.[7]

The significance of this is not the primacy of labour over capital as one in the eye for capital, but the central role that "the Catholic theory of the person" gives to human work. In principle, it is noble and ennobling because it is a human activity and, as such, worthy of unlimited respect. The dignity of labour requires it to be organised appropriately, lifting up the human spirit rather than grinding it down. Creativity is an energy – a God-given energy in the eye of believers – that the workplace organisation has to harness, in order to bring into existence that which did not exist before.

> *Work should never be reduced to the status of a mere instrument of production.*

How that creativity is harnessed is of course the challenge of good management; but this way of looking at it makes it clear that what is being harnessed is very precious, and should not be reduced to the status of a commodity. *Laborem Exercens* emphasises this by saying that work should never be reduced to the status of a mere instrument of production. So what makes work so significant is not the price that is paid for it or the use that is made of it but the fact it is done by human beings. *Laborem Exercens* puts it this way:

> The primary basis of the value of work is man himself, who is its subject. This leads immediately to a very important conclusion of an ethical nature: however true it may be that man is destined for work and called to it, in the first place work is for man and not man for work. Through this conclusion one rightly comes to recognize the pre-eminence of the subjective meaning of work over the objective one.

The statement that the "subjective meaning of work" takes precedence over the objective one might seem to suggest that the 'development' of the worker is of greater importance than the product of his work – that in effect the needs of producers should take precedence over the needs of consumers. This apparent weakness in the theory is overcome by the implicit emphasis through the encyclical both on 'vocation' and on creativity – the desire to give meaning to one's work by producing something of value to others. The 'excellence' that the worker strives for is not for the sake of pride or self-gratification, though job satisfaction is legitimate. It is for the sake of a service. Economically, excellence makes goods and services more desirable and therefore more profitable. But excellence always has much more to it than economic motivation; it has an emotional and moral quality described by such expressions as 'loving one's work'. It has an element of gratuitousness that is not so easily bought and sold.

Clearly, employers should regard their workforce as their greatest asset. It follows that in return, a workforce that is handled in a way compatible with its true dignity – 'treated like responsible human beings' – will make the greatest contribution to the success of the enterprise. That way the enterprise takes on the character of a shared exercise for whom everyone is responsible, and from whose success everyone benefits.

This brings the argument to the tricky question of moral character – do you have to be a good person to run a good business? How is this sort of goodness defined, and how is it acquired? Does it mean "goody" or just decent, honest and straight?

chapter 5 – references

1   Pope Francis, Apostolic Exhortation *Evangelii Gaudium* (2013).

2   www.blueprintforbusiness.org.

3   Ibid.

4   Ibid.

5   Pope John Paul II, *Laborem Exercens* (1981).

6   Throughout this discussion and elsewhere, he and his also means she and hers – though one of the major flaws of *Laborem Exercens* is that it still sees labour as a male activity, and the role of women is limited to that of wife and mother. Later Catholic Social Teaching documents are not quite so blinkered, though sadly none so far has approached work from a feminist perspective.

7   Lord (Maurice) Glasman, *The Crisis of Capitalism and the Politics of the Common Good* Margaret Beaufort Lecture, Cambridge 2011.

making a virtue of business

character versus regulation

Catholic Social Teaching documents praise virtue in the abstract, but rarely do they go further and say what they mean in detail. Similarly, secular calls for business activity to be conducted more 'morally' rarely specify what precise standards and values are assumed to be lacking from the business environment and which therefore need to be asserted. Such calls usually fail to make any practical suggestions that people engaged in business find relevant to their daily lives. Being told 'not to be greedy' is more irritating than helpful. And the whole concept of 'Business Ethics', particularly as an academic speciality but also as a provider of bearings for business people to steer by, is easily reduced to the status of a superficial add-on that does not go to the heart of the business operation.

Nevertheless its achievements include making it fashionable for businesses to have high-sounding 'mission statements' as well as to finance and run programmes under the name of Corporate Social Responsibility (CSR). There is no doubt they have had some success. The good causes which applied for and were granted funding under CSR were true beneficiaries. It was right that businesses accepted that they had public responsibilities, and that they should declare their intentions to act ethically and for the public good.

But mission statements and CSR were in fundamental tension with a business culture which took it as axiomatic that, in Milton Friedman's words, "the business of business is business" – that the singular purpose of business executives, and of the managers under them, was universally understood to be to maximise shareholder value, which meant making a profit that could be distributed to shareholders whilst bolstering the business's shareprice on the stock exchange so that holders of equity saw an increase in value. And because of this fundamental tension, mission statements and CSR programmes were easily seen – from within the business as much as from without – as window-dressing and exercises in public relations, or even as part of advertising and image-making. More cynically, they could be regarded as attempts to disguise the real purpose of business, making money, because that might not be viewed favourably by the public. In so far as this type of CSR approach cost money, it was accepted as the price to be paid in exchange for a favourable public perception. The more insidious danger is that CSR might be regarded as payback to the community to compensate it for activities that might be harmful to society, rather than addressing the nature of those activities so they cease to be harmful.

These initiatives have manifestly failed to alter the way business is conducted sufficiently to reverse the decline in public confidence and trust in business as a whole. According to an Ipsos MORI poll published in 2013, only 34 per cent of the public trusts business leaders to tell the truth compared with 57 per cent who do not.[1] This is about half the percentage when members of the public were asked to rate the truthfulness of the public in general (64 per cent vs. 26 per cent), a crude benchmark of "average" trustworthiness – but still considerably higher than the percentage of those who are prepared to trust the word of bankers (at 21 per cent vs. 75 per cent). Given that a broad cross-section of the public must include many who work in business, it is plain they do not trust each other. And it appears that levels of trust in most categories are falling year on year, with the most rapid falls in confidence among younger age groups.

There is a strong suggestion from such surveys that the public emphasises personal character rather than the nature of the business – the question of truthfulness referred to bankers as human beings, not banks as corporations. But the nature of the business – or rather how it operates – is highly relevant. If banks reward and promote certain types of performance by their staff, and the criteria for promotion put a low value on truth-telling, then that will shape the character of the people they employ as well as affecting the way they go about their daily business. For instance, if bank employees are financially rewarded to assure bank customers that mortgage protection insurance is good value and in their interests, yet they know that it is not, or at least are indifferent to whether it is or isn't, they are turned into habitual liars. They will lie about other things too. So it comes down to character – including the character of those in charge, who tolerate or encourage such practices.

Research by the Confederation of British Businesses (CBI) in association with Ipsos MORI, published in 2012, identified four key factors in the building of trust between the world of business and the public. The fourth recognised leadership, at all levels, as necessary to bring "a chosen set of values alive and to ensure delivery of these themes. Visible, respected leaders also provide figureheads for business, the public tend to trust individuals who they know and respect."[2]

There are problematic issues here. The mood among the public is not to expect business people to obey the rules and regulations by which business is governed, hence just to increase the volume or strictness of rules and regulations is unlikely to make an appreciable difference to trust. Tighter rules and regulations also come at a cost in efficiency, when business decisions have to be delayed while "compliance departments" – one of the faster growth sectors in the business economy – decide whether a particular proposal is within the rules or not. The public is not impressed to see key ethical decisions being sub-contracted to compliance specialists, whose expertise is usually in the interpretation of law, not moral philosophy. It is not surprising if the rest of the business operation quickly begins to feel like an ethics-free zone, and compliance itself becomes a game called "How far can we go?"

Despite the obvious drawbacks, increasing the emphasis on following and enforcing rules has become modern society's preferred official response to any evidence of moral failure, whether in business, in the professions, or more generally. But this is not universally true. One exception is the statement issued by the leaders of the Catholic Church in England and Wales, *Choosing the Common Good.*[3]

This document drew attention to the central importance of restoring and developing trust, both between individual businesses and in the relationship each business has with the wider community. It quoted *Caritas in Veritate* as stating that "development is impossible without upright men and women, without financiers and politicians whose consciences are finely attuned to the requirements of the common good", and added

> to act in this way requires more than not breaking rules. It demands the cultivation of moral character, the development of habits of behaviour which reflect a real respect for others and a desire to do good. It requires, in fact, the practice of virtue.

> Though supporters of neoliberalism advocate a minimum of regulations, it appears to be a paradoxical characteristic of that system that regulations inevitably multiply.

The problem with relying only on rules and regulations, it argues, is that the approach is inherently fragile and open to further abuses that require more and more regulations to meet them. Though supporters of neoliberalism advocate a minimum of regulations, it appears to be a paradoxical characteristic of that system that regulations inevitably multiply, because of the absence of a culture of virtue which could act as a check on inappropriate or harmful activities. This suggests that economists and particularly business leaders who wish to see less regulation need to cultivate virtue instead. A proliferation of regulations advertises a lack of trust.

This trade-off between regulation and virtue is implicitly recognised in the establishment of the Banking Standards Review Council, an "independent body that will promote high standards of behaviour and competence" in the financial sector, as its founder Sir Richard Lambert described it. Some commentators greeted news of the Council sceptically, suggesting it could never be more than a talking shop. Others suggest the financial sector may already be responding voluntarily, and does not need this extra pressure. But the general point remains valid. Lambert quoted Sir Andrew Large and Sir David Walker as warning, "if the industry does not volunteer standards…in areas where it knows that they could be effective, public officials have little alternative but to try to write rules".

The avoidance of inconvenience isn't the only issue. *Choosing the Common Good* observed that

> the practice of virtue helps to shape us as people. By the pursuit of virtue we act well not because of external constraint but because it has become natural for us to do so… It is doing good even when no-one is looking.

cardinal virtues

The document goes on to itemise the four major or 'cardinal'[4] virtues, giving a brief description of each. 'Prudence', or 'right reason in action', is the opposite of rashness and carelessness. It looks for what is good and asks how to achieve it. It is rational and intelligent, including emotional intelligence. In business, this is likely to mean finding the right balance between conflicting aims, which often requires a skilled judgement. Prudence is akin to wisdom; contrary to popular usage, it does not necessarily imply caution. A prudent financier may seize an opportunity for a daring investment.

'Courage' implies a readiness to stand by one's convictions. It is the opposite of opportunism and of evasiveness. It is the practice of fortitude in the face of difficulty, and it can produce heroism. Because it takes courage to try something new with unfamiliar hazards, it is a necessary virtue in the world of business enterprise, with the motto "nothing ventured, nothing gained". Courage enables a person to overcome irrational fears and to resist a consensus among colleagues which does not seem right. The first business person to say out loud 'profit isn't everything' may be surprised to discover how many people agree with him but haven't had the courage to say so. Courage is contagious, and a courageous person is often a natural leader prepared to walk ahead of the rest.

'Justice' means giving people what is their due, not just legally but morally, without wrangling. It is about performing duties and respecting rights. A worker who practises the virtue of justice will see that he owes an employer a fair day's work for a fair day's pay and will not take what is not his by right. A business manager who practices justice will see that debts are paid fully and on time, employees are treated fairly, their full contribution to the profitability of the enterprise is honoured, and that other stakeholders in the business will see their interests protected as far as possible. Justice can also be transgenerational –

the obligation to the future – and environmental – the duty to protect the natural world, locally and globally.

The virtue of 'temperance' or 'moderation' also creates obligations not to exhaust the resources of nature but to use them sustainably. Moderation in the market place means not being greedy and holding out for the last penny. While it means not taking too much it can also mean not taking too little. In remuneration it means knowing when enough is enough – and also when it is not enough. Both justice and temperance are therefore relevant to wage levels, which may not be set fairly by the market but which will need to take account of the right of an employee to enjoy a decent standard of living.

These Aristotelian virtues are both universal and secular, in that they relate to the relationships between human persons. Christianity would add three more, relating to the relationship with God, namely faith, hope and charity (*caritas*), and although some might claim justice is greater than and obviates the need for charity, this is a false contrast. In the words of *Caritas in Veritate*:

> Charity goes beyond justice, because to love is to give, to offer what is 'mine' to the other; but it never lacks justice, which prompts us to give the other what is 'his', what is due to him by reason of his being or his acting. I cannot 'give' what is mine to the other, without first giving him what pertains to him in justice... Justice is the primary way of charity.

the 'practice' within the 'institution'

The key to understanding the concept of virtue is character formation. Aristotle's insight was that people learn certain behaviour by copying others and by repetition; it becomes habitual. If that behaviour is virtuous, making it a habit means internalising it so that virtue becomes part of that person's nature. It is how they react without conscious thought. A person with the virtue of courage who sees an infant fall on a railway track will not delay rescuing the child while he makes rational calculations and conducts a cost-benefit analysis. He will act as if from instinct. Prudence may tell him the approaching train is too near and there is no hope. But again those decisions will be spontaneous. He will be acting in character.

Work in the field of virtue ethics by the Scottish philosopher Alasdair MacIntyre, who is a Catholic and who works in the Aristotelian and Thomistic tradition, has deepened the understanding of the role of virtue and how it is shaped by (and sometimes captured by) institutions.[5] One of MacIntyre's insights was that modern Western culture still contains substantial vestiges of any older moral order. It may be out of fashion among academic philosophers, but the population at large still uses these ideas to express its values.

MacIntyre makes a key distinction between 'practices' and 'institutions'. A practice is an activity which requires skill and implies a commitment to the value of that skill. One word to describe that attitude would be 'vocation'. Medicine would be a good example of a vocational practice in this MacIntyrean sense. In the business world, the first example given by Professor John Kay from ICI's 1987 annual report would be another example of this kind of practice, referring to the vocation of the scientist, and to the value of what he or she did, to advance the common good.

A hospital or clinic would be a good example of an institution in which medicine is practised. Doctors could go about fulfilling their vocation to heal the sick without any support or administrative back-up whatever, and if they found themselves dealing with someone who had collapsed in the street, they would have to do so. But normally the work of doctors requires a host of ancillary services – heating, lighting and accommodation, clerical staff to marshal patients and book appointments, someone to keep records, a supply of drugs, a facility for blood tests, x-rays and so on; and some way of paying for it all. All these require the existence of an institution. In an ideal world, the purpose of the institution is to provide the setting in which the practise of medicine can go on. Similarly, ICI as a corporate structure existed to provide the setting in which science could go on. To use another example that MacIntyre uses, a chess club is an institution, chess itself is a practice.

Within a practice, the aim of the practitioner is the pursuit of excellence. It is that which marks it as a vocation. This requires the deployment of virtue, which has excellence as its primary object. The virtues in question may be Plato's four,[6] the so-called cardinal virtues (prudence, temperance, justice and courage) as they are the ones on which other virtues hinge, plus St Paul's three (faith, hope and charity), but also virtues specific to excellence in medicine, chess or science. The aim of the institution, on the other hand, ought to be to enable and allow the practice, which might not otherwise be possible on any organised or enduring scale.

Central to MacIntyre's analysis is his recognition of the tendency of institutions to acquire other less honourable objectives. In a free market system, though profit is necessary if a business is to stay afloat, those other ends are usually to do with making money. John Kay's ICI example discussed in Chapter 1 shows that actually happening. The later statement of the company's aim showed how the institution had by 1994 acquired an aim different from 1987's "serving customers internationally," namely "to maximise value for our shareholders." Indirectly, that abandonment of the pursuit of excellence in the practice of science meant the end of the idea of virtue and the concept of vocation. Science became a means to another end.

This example comes from industry, though it also records a change that some have called "financialisation", describing the way purely financial criteria have taken over from industrial criteria. It describes the way the industrial sector of the economy, with an industrial set of values, is being colonised by the financial sector, so that financial sector values – essentially the set of ideas contained in neoliberalism – are gradually being substituted. Not all firms are equally affected, and the relationship between the financial economy and the so-called 'real economy' has become a live issue in the business world, with many business leaders regretting the way the latter is sucked into the former. This is acutely experienced when industrial firms are the subject of mergers or takeovers for reason of financial engineering, and it is also reflected in the way industrial companies are themselves regarded as tradable commodities that can be bought and sold for profit or to gain tax advantages.

The financial sector itself as it now exists is the product of a similar cultural change. It was once seen as a vocation and its practitioners as people of moral standing. Bank managers were the most solid of citizens, playing an active part within local society in every role from magistrates and school governors to stalwart members of the local Rotary group or masonic lodge. They were respected because they knew their communities, to which they provided financial facilities like loans and overdrafts as a service to the public and to commerce. Their basic skills were the making of moral judgements – assessing credit worthiness, who to trust and who not to; who to help, who to advise and who to avoid. Making moral judgments required that they themselves practised virtue, and understood moral character. The fact that Ipsos MORI records bankers as about the least trusted of all professions reveals what has happened since. Banking as a practice – the City of London prided itself on being a place where people could say to each other 'my word is my bond' – has been captured by banking as an institution, whose single purpose is to make money – often by sailing as close to the wind as an individual may dare. Bankers have sacrificed their moral status in society, in the name of maximising shareholder value. Ideology has trumped morality.

This is an example of a 'practice', to use MacIntyre's term to describe what the vocation of financier is about, being captured by an institution, or indeed by all the institutions in the financial sector acting as one under the banner of neoliberal ideology. In fact banking, investing, managing an enterprise, accounting, and all the other skills needed by a modern business enterprise can all be counted as vocational practices in the MacIntyrean sense, and therefore can all be done virtuously in pursuit of excellence. That is what is meant by the title of the Vatican document referred to in Chapter 1, *The Vocation of the Business Leader.*

If virtue is no longer prized in business because it is not relevant to that core purpose, an inevitable amorality descends over the rest of it. And an amoral world containing people who have given up on virtue is likely to be a breeding ground for vice – an archaic term to introduce into the business environment, but as a term for the opposite of virtue there is no other. In the light of a whole series of unsavoury revelations in the financial sector such as the Libor-fixing scandal, it seems fair to say that the environment has now degenerated to the point where vice, dishonest behaviour, is no longer surprising. As Reuters' financial reporting service wrote in 2013,

> US and European regulators fined banks record amounts this year, imposing penalties and settlements of more than $43 billion as authorities work more closely across borders to clean up the financial sector.[7]

There are those who say the more unregulated a free market, the more efficient it is; hence the more profitable. But when being free both of external regulation and of an internal culture of moral values can lead to penalties in one year of this astronomical order of magnitude, the question naturally arises – what are the alternatives?

chapter 6 – references

1   Ipsos MORI Trust Poll http://www.ipsos-mori.com/Assets/Docs/Polls/Feb2013_Trust_Topline. PDF 15 February 2013.

2   Drivers of Trust in Business: www.cbi.org.uk/campaigns/business-consumers-and-communities/how-business-contributes-to-society/drivers-of-trust-in-business/

3   *Choosing the Common Good* Catholic Bishops' Conference of England and Wales (2010).

4   Comes from the Latin *cardo*, hinge, as all the other virtues turn upon these four.

5   Alasdair MacIntyre, *After Virtue* (Bloomsbury, 1981).

6   Aristotle in his *Rhetoric* offers five extra: magnificence, magnanimity, liberality, gentleness, wisdom.

7   Steve Slater, 'Banks pay for past sins as U.S., Europe levy record fines', *Reuters Financial Reporting Service* 24 December 2013 http://www.reuters.com/article/2013/12/24/us-banks-fines-idUSBRE9BN00I20131224

"it's not about the money"

social market, Keynes – or MacIntyre?

Catholic Social Teaching does not claim to be an economic theory in itself, but provides a commentary on other theories. That might look like a strength, but in the present circumstances it can be a weakness. It criticizes economic systems such as neoliberalism that promote the single object of maximising profit. But in some economies, neoliberal profit maximisation is the only show in town. Those who criticise it have also to show that an alternative is possible; otherwise neoliberalism wins by default. It may be a bad system but if it is the only possible system, we're stuck with it. That would apply even if the theory has fundamental flaws which predestine it to repeat its mistakes in a never ending cycle of crises.

Can Catholic Social Teaching be used to construct an alternative to neoliberalism? The German social market model, also followed in many other European economies, is an obvious candidate. Part of the reason for the ongoing tension between Britain and the European Union is the mismatch of economic models. The EU is more inclined than Britain to use economic theory to produce social goals – more orientated towards the common good. The Social Chapter of the Maastricht Treaty in 1992, from which the Major Government negotiated an opt-out, is an example of this disparity. Nevertheless the German experience has not been an unqualified success, and the German version of the Welfare State may have as many holes as the British one. Furthermore some commentators have seen signs that neoliberalism has been gaining some hold among German economists including on the centre-left.[1] Rather than adopt the German model, as some suggest, it might be better to return to the first principles on which the German model was based, and make use of them afresh.

Many British business leaders are pragmatists, and many British businesses are run on lines that fall short of (or are morally superior to, depending on your point of view) the neoliberal ideal. They may say one thing to fund managers, whose preoccupation with share price movements is legendary, and another thing for internal consumption. They balance as best they can – and as decency and common sense require – the interests of shareholders and of other stakeholders, not just employees but customers, suppliers and the wider community.

Nevertheless pragmatism has its limits. Some clear framework of ideas may be necessary to give the necessary confidence to encourage change to a more holistic conception of the business enterprise. There are many signs that the business world is searching for such a philosophy, many initiatives springing up (*Blueprint for a Better Business* is one already mentioned), many seminars and conferences convened to exchange ideas.

vocation, virtue and excellence

One possibility would be a deeper embrace of Keynesianism, although many question whether Keynesianism is enough. Maurice Glasman puts it this way:

> The theoretical predicament is that on their own, neither a Keynesian nor a neoclassical approach can grasp the importance of institutions; of vocation, virtue and value in generating competitive advantage, reciprocity as the foundation of good practice and the importance of long-term relationships between capital, labour and place in generating growth and innovation.[2]

Glasman goes on to point out that it was these institutions and practices that underlay the comparative strength of the post-war German political-economy. This did not pursue a Keynesian model, but one "based on worker representation in firms, a vocational economy and robust regional banks constrained to lend within the region or the sector." The consequence was (and is) a German economy with better vocational training and longer apprenticeships, higher wages, higher levels of skill, greater productivity and greater international competitiveness than the United Kingdom has seen. The attitude to 'work' is key.

A new economic settlement that was grounded in Catholic Social Teaching would, thus, start not with capital but with labour. It would agree with the predominant CST idea that in the creation of wealth, both labour and capital are necessary, but that labour is human whereas capital is material, and therefore takes precedence. It would avoid the Marxist trap, however, of assuming that the interests of capital and the interests of labour cannot be reconciled. It is in the interest of both capital and labour that they should be. There is no inevitable failure awaiting such efforts, as Marxists would predict, provided both sides see the need for mutual accommodation to the advantage of each. Without labour, capital just sits there doing nothing; without capital, labour either starves to death or drowns in debt.

This is where MacIntyrean virtue ethics can make a major contribution. Wealth creation, the ultimate basis for profit, happens whenever value is added to a product or service, whether by turning a chunk of metal into a motorcar or tailoring the conditions of a house mortgage to suit the exact requirements of lender and borrower. Such processes demand skills that have to be learnt, first in theory and then in practice. Practice means not just learning by repetition, but being absorbed in and committed to the pursuit of excellence – doing the job as well as it can be done.[3]

In MacIntyrean ethics, excellence in the practice is an end in itself, and excellence requires what he calls virtue. A craft has to be studied and learnt, its innate disciplines and challenges mastered; manual and mental skills have to be coordinated, and the practitioner has to acquire an underlying sense of what the practice demands. He inhabits a culture conditioned by other practitioners, and he inherits a tradition of practical virtue on which he draws and to which he contributes. One element in it will inevitably be ethical – there are things a good practitioner would not do as they contradict the essence of the craft. The policing of this ethos will be both personal and collective. He even takes his identity from the practice – he becomes a dentist, a road sweeper, cobbler or an architect, and continues to be that person even at rest.

If he has a particular talent for it or a love of the craft, whether he is talented or not, it is right to talk of this practice as his vocation. It is something he is called upon to be (by God, Nature or Fate) and to do. However modest or difficult, it is the way he fulfils his capability. The Catholic Social Teaching's theory of work tells us that vocation is universal. Everyone has one. One of the most important skills of management is to ensure that every job in the workforce has the potential to enhance human dignity rather than to degrade it. Work that is felt by the worker to be worthwhile will not only feel more satisfying but be better performed.

This applies whatever the level of skill. There is a clumsy way of sweeping a street or ironing a shirt, and an excellent way. Whatever the job, a good worker takes pride in it. Doing it will give him satisfaction. There is true nobility in basic manual work, a lesson Europe learnt from the monks of the Benedictine order – motto "work and pray" – and has since been largely forgotten. The low estimation of the dignity of work, and of those who do it is one of the factors behind low pay and such growing practices as zero-hours contracts. It may be to escape from this low estimation of work and the lack of respect that comes with it, that one of the major trends in the British economy is the growth of self-employment.

The theory of work contained in Catholic Social Teaching also breaks down the distinctions between paid and unpaid work, sometimes unsatisfactorily described as a pastime or hobby. Gardening is gardening whether paid or unpaid. Housework is housework. And it breaks down the distinction between professionals and tradesmen. They are simply at different levels within similar practices; both levels are necessary.

Vocational education is vital, in developing skill at the practice and in developing the character formation that lies behind it. For instance this extract from the Mission Statement of the BRIT School in Croydon, the place which nurtured the talents of a range of performing artists such as Adele Watkins, Leona Lewis, Amy Winehouse and Jessie J, expresses these truths precisely:

> The BRIT School for the Performing Arts and Technology aims to provide a high quality education for 14 to 19-year-olds through a specialist curriculum. Performing and creative arts with their related technologies are at its core and contribute to a curriculum aimed at developing the whole person.
>
> We aim to develop students academically, vocationally, socially and morally so that they leave the School as independent, co-operative, responsible and creative young people with a lifelong interest and ability in learning, the arts, technology and self-development.[4]

There is no mention of fame and fortune among the objectives that students at the BRIT School might set themselves (or, to quote Jessie J herself, "It's not about the money money money…") Many educational institutions may claim to have similar lofty ambitions, yet one of the most persistent complaints from educationalists is the way universities and colleges are being turned into businesses. In other words, they are succumbing to an all-pervading ideology which not only undermines their own pursuit of excellence but conditions young people to see the world exclusively in terms of financial success. So the ideology is capturing the institution, and the institution is capturing the practice.

The relationship between artistic success and wealth is complex – supporting John Kay's theory in his book *Obliquity* that some goals can only be achieved by not aiming directly at them. The MacIntyrean truth would seem to be: pursue excellence, and wealth may follow; but more importantly still, so may happiness and personal fulfilment.

Practice, whether music and the performing arts or any other, requires an institutional framework. The BRIT School itself is one such; the relevant practice there is the teaching of the performing arts and helping students to reach excellence. The proper function of the institution is to allow optimum conditions for the pursuit of that practice to the highest level. But the institution must also survive in the real world: it must have an income to live on, and capital for accommodation and equipment. The BRIT School is technically in the public sector, supported by the state and the entertainment industry. In the private sector, an institution needs to make a profit and attract shareholders to invest. But as Alasdair

MacIntyre points out, it is all too easy for the institution's need to make a profit to crowd out other purposes, in effect to 'capture' the practices so they become subordinate to this primary objective. In fact that can prove toxic to the practice as it ends up torn between two masters, profit and excellence, which may well not be compatible.

Yet the pursuit of excellence by practitioners is necessarily at the heart of the wealth creation process, without which there would be no profits. However, if the interests of shareholders come first, subordinating the needs of wealth-creating practice to the demands of the profit-making institution, those same interests are undermined. The secret of the profit-making alchemy is lost. This is the lesson of the ICI story that John Kay told in Chapter 1, and it is the fatal paradox of neoliberalism.

The Mission Statement of the BRIT School is fully compliant with what *Laborem Exercens* has to say about the role of work in human fulfilment, which comes about through respecting the full human dignity of the worker, including the essential element of creativity. There are many secular versions of the same insights, though they tend to be instrumental in an economic sense – contented employees make a business more profitable – rather than focusing on the humanity of the worker which is, in Catholic Social Teaching, ultimately what work is all about. As a human being is made in the image of God the Creator, a human being is also a creator – and in the same sense.

In a report by the Work Foundation in 2012, Professor Stephen Bevan, Director of the Centre for Workforce Effectiveness, argued that there are four primary conditions of what might be called 'good work'.[5] The key is 'engagement', the sense of a genuine participation and involvement in what the worker is doing. The evidence shows that engagement among British workers is significantly lower than in other industrialised countries. On promoting engagement, he says:

> Making the connection to the purpose of the organisation, and their part in it, is the basis of engaging employees' best efforts – i.e. elevating it above a mechanistic set of processes designed to deliver 'employee engagement', to focus on what makes the whole enterprise meaningful. Make engagement mean something more than just a staff survey score.[6]

"The established business case for employee engagement is a win: win," he continues,

> resulting in improved performance and productivity for employers and a better experience for work employees – and creating a committed and engaged workforce requires being honest about the time and resources you invest in managing a complex mix of factors.

His recipe includes flexibility – giving employees scope to manage their time better, including the balance between life at home and at work; autonomy – providing a level of self-governance over how they do their job; giving employees a voice so they are involved in decisions which affect them and feel a sense of participation in the whole organisation; and aiding development and personal growth by offering the opportunity to learn new things and to progress in their working life. Professor Bevan goes on to comment that

> the experience of work on a day-to-day basis is not what is captured in the formal contract, but is implicit in the expectations, processes, values and relationships in the workplace.

gift and reciprocity

This reference to going beyond the formal terms of an employment contract resonates with another, and relatively new, insight of Catholic Social Teaching, the importance of 'gift' – what the encyclical *Caritas in Veritate* calls gratuitousness, reciprocity and fraternity. They are characteristic of civil society – the lifeblood of which is freely given service – but they are not to be excluded from economic life. The encyclical says:

> The Church's social doctrine holds that authentically human social relationships of friendship, solidarity and reciprocity can also be conducted within economic activity, and not only outside it or 'after' it… In commercial relationships the principle of gratuitousness and the logic of gift as an expression of fraternity can and must find their place within normal economic activity.

A worker committed to his work will seek excellence for its own sake and for the satisfaction it brings, which will generally mean doing more than the minimum required by his employment contract. That which is over and above the minimum is what *Caritas in Veritate* means by "gift". There is no deal, no exchange of equivalents, but nevertheless the idea remains essential if work is to be a fully human activity. In Catholic Social Teaching that is understood as employees feeling "in a certain sense" (*Laborem Exercens*) that they are working for themselves as well as for their employer.

The idea of gift lies within a wider ecology of reciprocity. A courteous person may open a door for someone carrying a heavy load – a gratuitous act – with no expectation that the next day the roles will be reversed and the favour repaid. But in due course a similar favour might be done for him by someone else: such acts go into a kind of common pool of favours, which may be drawn upon by others in due course. This, in turn, breeds trust. People see other people acting decently towards one another, and that creates an expectation of decency all round. It becomes possible to rely on the word of someone who one knows is decent. Thus the element of gratuitousness naturally builds trust. And this is fundamental to creating a working environment in which people feel comfortable.

Matthew Taylor, director of the Royal Society of Arts, remarked in a lecture in 2013 that the widespread lack of engagement by workers in the work they do in Britain had serious economic consequences.

> Researchers and businesses are increasingly seeing how central engagement is not only to organisational and economic success, but also a range of wider benefits... The Chartered Institute of Personnel and Development estimates that disengaged employees take more than twice as many sick days as engaged employees. Estimates vary, but there is no doubt that reducing the number of actively disengaged workers, or increasing the number of actively engaged, could add tens of billions of pounds to the country's GDP.[7]

This is seriously good news for any new economic model that is grounded in Catholic Social Teaching, for it suggests that such a model could out-perform the neoliberal model quite significantly, in strictly economic terms. That one would out-perform the other in human terms is obvious.

chapter 7 – references

1   Ashley Lavelle, 'Social Democracy or Neo-liberalism?' in *Globalising Government Business Relations* (Pearson Education Australia, 2007).

2   Maurice Glasman, 'We Need to Talk about Keynes – and his Viagra Economics' *The Guardian* 8 July 2012.

3   See Alasdair MacIntyre, *After Virtue* (Bloomsbury, 1981) and subsequent titles. However MacIntyre nowhere supports the idea that capitalism is redeemable, either by the application of virtue ethics or any other means. Such an interpretation is the author's, not his.

4   'About Us', The BRIT School website, http://www.brit.croydon.sch.uk/page/?title= About+Us&pid=6 (2014)

5   Stephen Bevan, *Good Work, High Performance and Productivity* (Work Foundation, 2012); www.theworkfoundation.com/downloadpublication/report/316_ goodworkhighperformanceandproductivity.pdf

6   ibid.

7   Matthew Taylor *Getting Engaged* RSA Journal Issue 4, 2013 http://www.thersa.org/large-text/ fellowship/journal/archive/issue-4-2013/features/getting-engaged

bonus culture

how neoliberalism rewards the wrong things

The existing economic model is structured by law and by practice towards the goal of maximising shareholder value, and treats philosophical questions concerning employment, like those we have been discussing, as marginal or irrelevant. Thus senior executives are remunerated exclusively on the basis of short-term profit and share price, not on whether the conditions of employment are such as to maximise the value a worker can contribute to a firm, nor – and here reciprocity is crucial – to maximise the value that the firm can contribute to the employee.

The very idea is likely to produce blank faces round the boardroom table. Executives are not normally engaged with employment questions except when there is trouble. Indeed, the modern executive is often an accountant by profession – more than half of the current chief executives of companies in the FTSE 100 have a background in accountancy or financial management[1] – and is deemed to have transferable skills that are as relevant to the business of managing one company as to any other, regardless of the nature of the core business.

That means, however, that they are ill-equipped to understand what are in MacIntyrean terms the essential practices that the firm exists to promote if it is to succeed. A modern engineering company might have no engineers on the board, a chemical company no chemists. The necessary skills have all been 'financialised'. But the management of trade and professional practices to get the best out of them is itself a practice requiring great skill and a good understanding of what the particular practice entails, as well as all the professional virtues that help to build trust.

Catholic Social Teaching has always pointed to the existence in any business of other stakeholders than shareholders. As *Caritas in Veritate* declares,

> business management cannot concern itself only with the interests of the proprietors, but must also assume responsibility for all the other stakeholders

who contribute to the life of the business: the workers, the clients, the suppliers of various elements of production, the community of reference.

The high-point of the stakeholder movement in British business is probably represented by the reform of the Companies Act in 2006, and the failure of that reform to deliver much of anything may explain the subsequent decline in interest.

Clause 172 of the Act states that the duty of a company director is to act in good faith

to promote the success of the company for the benefit of its members as a whole, and in doing so have regard (amongst other matters) to –

(a) the likely consequences of any decision in the long term,

(b) the interests of the company's employees,

(c) the need to foster the company's business relationships with suppliers, customers and others,

(d) the impact of the company's operations on the community and the environment,

(e) the desirability of the company maintaining a reputation for high standards of business conduct, and

(f) the need to act fairly as between members of the company.[2]

Official guidance indicated that "having regard to" meant "thinking about".

Obviously this did not usher in a new age of industrial democracy, as for instance practised in Germany. Catholic Social Teaching does not actually advocate any particular pattern of industrial democracy, but it does go further than sub-clause (b). In practice while board members may have to "think about" the interests of workers under this clause, they are not obliged to consult them as to where they think their interests lie, nor are they open to challenge. Indeed a board member who accepts uncritically the Milton Friedman line that "the business of business is business" is entitled to discharge his duty under this Clause 172 by saying that whatever is in the interest of shareholders must inevitably, in the long or short run, be in the interest of all other stakeholders. In any event, the board are not answerable to all the stakeholders for how they discharge their duties under Clause 172, only to the one group that elects them, namely the shareholders – who are unlikely to unseat a board member for giving priority to themselves over other stakeholders. Whatever may have been the intentions of the legislators, British company law still remains a reflection of neoliberal economic theory.

This is not necessarily difficult to fix. A simple rewording of the first part of Clause 172, changing the duty of directors from a permissive "in doing so have regard (amongst other matters) to…" to the more prescriptive "by having regard to…" (leaving out "other matters" as too vague for a legal duty) would transform the boardroom conversation from being about maximising shareholder value to being about serving the common good, represented by all the interests the Clause goes on to list.

A legal right of employees to buy and own shares (with voting rights) in the company that employs them, and a reserved place for their representative director at the boardroom table, is not inconceivable nor alarmingly radical. This is not so much surrender to Karl Marx as judicious borrowing from the example of John Lewis. But it would enable the board to have direct access to those engaged in the craft and professional practices that are at the heart of the business, and to become conscious of the conditions under which they flourish. A further reform that would switch business from the debilitating emphasis on short-term profit maximisation to the real mechanics of wealth creation would be to abolish the custom – regarded by many businessmen as almost mandatory – of quarterly reporting on the state of the business to the stock markets. It is a demand of investment managers, but it is to the detriment of the economy on whose flourishing they depend.

letting in the other stakeholders

One 'interest' that directors are required to consider under company law is described as the environment (see sub-clause (d) above). But whereas a company has a commercial and contractual relationships with employers, consumers and suppliers, there is no equivalent entity pressing the case for the ecological factors which a company's activities might disturb. There are outside campaigning or lobby groups, but (d) gives them no right to be heard. The slight rewording of Clause 172 suggested above would also make it a necessary part of a company director's duty to consider and weigh environmental impacts, and not just vaguely "think about" them. In other words they would have to take responsibility for their effect on the environment.

There is inevitable resistance to the idea of industrial democracy *per se* or indeed to any role for workers as stakeholders, if that simply means letting trades union representatives into the boardroom. They are presumed to be an 'interest' automatically opposed to the interests of shareholders. Though sophisticated trades union leaders nowadays stress that industrial democracy means partnership and collaboration, decades of both sides treating the relationship between employees and managers as a locus of class war between capital and labour – incidentally an interpretation always strongly resisted by Catholic Social Teaching – have left permanent scars on both sides. If managers see trades unions as 'the enemy' then industrial democracy sounds like an attempt to undermine the fortress from within.

In German company law, co-determination means that in companies with more than 2,000 employees, half of a supervisory board of directors, which elects managers, has to be elected by shareholders and the other half by workers, with a shareholder representative as chairman. This is the case whether the workplace is unionised or not; and where they are, directors elected by the workforce are answerable to them and not to a union. The evidence suggests that the involvement of workers in decision-making under co-determination leads to increased productivity and a more motivated and happier workforce, with less absenteeism and lower likelihood of strikes. Co-determination was introduced under the inspiration of Catholic Social Teaching as a deliberate attempt to move beyond a simple clash of interests in the workplace and to emphasise collaboration and shared responsibility between workers and managers. The biggest single obstacle to the reform of company governance in Britain to take advantage of co-determination is undoubtedly the prevalence of neoliberal ideology, which sees it as a distraction from the Milton Friedman formula that "the business of business is business".

There are other obstacles. Many trade unionists prefer to advance the interest of their members – seen almost wholly in financial terms – by traditional negotiation, with the threat of industrial action in the background. Indeed, Catholic Social Teaching accepts that model, defends the right of unions to exist and of employees to join them, and defends the right to strike. In various parts of Europe in the twentieth century, trades unions of Catholic workers were specifically formed from time to time in order to compete with and confront communist trades unions – a course of action directly advocated by *Rerum Novarum*.

Hence present company structures have a deficit from the point of view of Catholic Social Teaching, in that the relationship between employees and the company is not a natural one but is distorted by the neoliberal imperative to maximise shareholder value. Indeed, it is further distorted by the way the remuneration of directors is linked to shareholder value by a system of share options and bonuses. These were introduced to correct a tendency for managers to act as a law unto themselves, by giving them a direct interest in line with the interests of shareholders. But it has inevitably led to the manipulation of shareholder value in order to enrich the directors. Thus the larger a company is, the higher the pay of its executives – and the greater the incentive, therefore, to grow a company by mergers and acquisitions even when that enlargement brings no obvious benefit to shareholders. Similarly, some boards of directors have come to measure their company's virility by the size of the CEO's compensation package, leading to a kind of competition between companies to see who can pay the most.

Company neoliberalism is seen at its most extortionate when it is invoked to justify huge payments to executives because otherwise they would leave and go to work elsewhere. It is a system with an inbuilt ratchet. It can only go one way – upwards – and each rise triggers further rises elsewhere in order to keep pace. This has now become a significant driver of inequality. Economists are divided over whether Thomas Piketty, in his *Capital in the Twenty-First Century*, has proved his case that capitalism overall is an inevitable engine of ever-greater inequality. But the way the bonus culture has succeeded in enriching an already wealthy elite is powerful evidence in his favour.

wages not the enemy of profit

Neoliberalism is a system which, at the other end of the scale, necessarily reduces employees to mere units of labour, and labour itself to a commodity to be bought and sold, subject to market forces in the so-called labour market. In reality human beings refuse to behave according to the law of supply and demand, which results repeatedly in economists' predictions being confounded. It was widely and confidently predicted for instance that the introduction of the minimum wage in Britain after the 1997 General Election would increase unemployment, by, according to some sources, as many as a million. Nothing like that happened. Cuts in public spending after the 2010 General Election were also predicted to cause a large increase in unemployment, and again the figure of a million was mentioned. That didn't happen either. Chris Giles, writing in the *Financial Times*, stated:

> Britain's labour market has behaved in ways that no one expected ever since the crisis unfolded. Unemployment rose much less than expected, public sector job cuts have been greater, employment has risen higher than the previous peak, yet wage growth has remained extremely weak and there is significant evidence that people would work more hours if they could.[3]

Yet it is a measure of the extent to which neoliberal ideas have become entrenched in British political debate, that any attempt to interfere in the balance between supply and demand in the labour market is declared to be gravely detrimental to both sides, and in the long run, ineffective. In neoliberal thinking, the activity of trades unions in trying to change the outcome of market forces with regard to wages is bound to lead to inefficiency and hence lower profits for business, and fewer jobs for workers. Market forces cannot be bucked, it is assumed. But events prove they can be. Indeed, every single individual in the national workforce may be regarded as engaged in a personal battle to outwit market forces, at least in their own case.

Nowhere is this counter-intuitive behaviour of the labour market more manifest than with regard to the "living wage". The idea became popular after a local campaign to shame well-paid business executives into giving the cleaners who cleaned their offices in Canary Wharf, East London, an income above the miserly minimum they were then being paid.

The campaign, which developed out of the work of the Zacchaeus 2000 Trust, was taken up by successive Labour and Conservative Mayors of London, Ken Livingstone and Boris Johnson, in the form of a 'London living wage' – set above the national living wage because life in the capital is more expensive. In pure free market terms, raising wages above the level they needed to be at, to satisfy the requirements of supply and demand, should lead to unemployment. But once again, labour markets did not behave like proper markets are supposed to.

Catholic churches in the East End of London were particularly active in the early days of the living wage campaign, a campaign which was taken up by the powerful grass roots social activism organisation London Citizens. (Catholic churches in southern Chicago were similarly involved in corresponding social activism, providing an environment where a young Barack Obama first learnt his political skills as a community organiser.)[4] This is not surprising. Catholic Social Teaching puts special emphasis on the so called "preferential option for the poor", an idea first coined by Liberation Theology in South America and now given new urgency under the papacy of Pope Francis.

It means that any social and political agenda has to give particular weight to the interests of the least powerful groups in society – children, the poor, the infirm, the disabled, the vulnerable, or indeed anyone excluded – precisely because they are not able to exert political or economic pressure on their own behalf. 'Giving weight to them' means addressing the fundamental causes of their problems, which are almost invariably bound up with the various forms of poverty. In the words of Pope Francis:

> As long as the problems of the poor are not radically resolved by rejecting the absolute autonomy of markets and financial speculation and by attacking the structural causes of inequality, no solution will be found for the world's problems or, for that matter, to any problems. Inequality is the root of social ills.[5]

It is not just citizens' groups and community organisers who see the benefits of a living wage. The business consultants KPMG were early adopters of the living wage in their own affairs, and they reported it "simply makes good business sense":

> Since introducing the Living Wage for its staff in 2006, KPMG has found that the extra wage costs are more than met by lowered recruitment churn and absenteeism, greater loyalty, and higher morale leading to better performance.

Turnover amongst KPMG's contracted cleaning staff has more than halved since paying the Living Wage.[6]

KPMG's own research bears out that this is also the experience of other living wage employers. The fundamental values of Catholic Social Teaching say that if you treat people like human beings, they start to behave like human beings.

> *The fundamental values of Catholic Social Teaching say that if you treat people like human beings, they start to behave like human beings.*

In the lecture already referred to, Matthew Taylor of the RSA drew the lessons. "If managers accept that robust employee engagement has to include representation and voice," he said,

> and if the champions of workers recognise that most employees see no inherent conflict between their interest and those of their organisation, we may be able to aim for a full sense of engagement at work to be the experience of the majority, not just the lucky minority.

He continued:

> But this framework should not overshadow the importance of individual aspiration or responsibility. Survey after survey shows that one of the key determinants of whether we enjoy work is the degree of autonomy and discretion we feel we have in our jobs… We can hardly expect human dignity and fulfilment – which is ultimately the measure of better work – if we do not ourselves seek it. Reform and innovation will only come about if we as workers move beyond an instrumental or fatalistic attitude to our jobs. Good for us, good for organisations and good for our country: better work should be everyone's business.[7]

Thus, Matthew Taylor, himself not a Catholic, sums up what a post-neoliberal political economy might look like if it took seriously the criteria of Catholic Social Teaching – criteria which he himself would also ground in post-Enlightenment secular humanism.

neoliberalism versus the common good

Few would disagree that the promotion of "integral human development" of everyone on the planet was a worthy aim; or that the "full human dignity" of every person ought to be respected. Few would disagree, also, that these are values we share and ought to be committed to, as far as we are able – in other words, they are our "common good". It follows that every economic system or theory that offers itself for our approval ought to be submitted to the simple test: does it foster these basic human values, or hinder them? What does it say about the common good? Those are the criteria supplied by Catholic Social Teaching to this debate.

Neoliberalism undoubtedly has the capacity to generate great wealth, but it also has, as 2007-2008 manifestly demonstrated, an even greater capacity to destroy it. It also appears to have a strong tendency to reward the wealthy – those who already have capital – without an equal tendency to reward those whose contribution to the creation of wealth is through their work. That inevitably creates tensions that are in opposition to the common good. They weaken the cohesion of society by undermining trust. They advertise all too loudly that we are not 'all in this together.'

The dangers inherent in growing inequality were highlighted in Christine Lagarde's address to the Inclusive Capitalism conference already mentioned. She said:

> The principles of solidarity and reciprocity that you see celebrated in many encyclicals from Leo XIII to our Pope Francis that bind societies together are more likely to erode in excessively unequal societies. Pope Francis recently put this in stark terms when he called increasing inequality 'the root of social evil'.[8]

There is a natural tendency for governments, on seeing businesses operating without internal constraints, with all the danger to the common good that that brings with it as 2008 showed, to make good the deficiency by imposing binding external constraints – regulations. Hence neoliberalism breeds the expansion regulation, almost to the same degree that it hates it. The regulatory burden generates costs which lower efficiency and reduce profits. But it has another, more insidious effect. Regulations crowd out virtue. Business persons who might well want to conduct their affairs in accordance with the common good get no credit for it.

Instead, their only goal becomes 'compliance'. Instead of asking 'Is this right or wrong?' they are required to ask 'Is this within the rules or not?' And they are likely to have to ask that of other people rather than themselves, as compliance turns on legal interpretations and past precedents which require specialist knowledge that is continuously updated. Increasing regulation inevitably undermines the very standards the regulations are designed to police. Though they are meant to restore trust, in practice they destroy it.

An economic system which answers to the common good, in other words which accepts internal moral restraints on its ability to make profits, would be more trustworthy and actually require less regulation. It would generate those moral restraints itself, because it would have an internal structure and culture that was infused with moral and ethical principles – and, in doing so, would be more, not less, efficient.

You might well ask where it would get these principles from, and the answer appears to be from the background values of society at large, from civil society – the space where most of us spend most of our lives. That includes, of course, the most important generators and custodians of moral values within civil society, who are the creators of the particular form of wealth called moral capital – namely the churches and other institutions of religion, which devote themselves to the worship of God and to asking themselves the great question, the only one that matters to them: how does God want me to live my life?

The moral capital they protect and generate – primarily visible in the form of trust – is just as important to the success of businesses as the physical capital they need – money. To quote Christine Lagarde again:

> The behaviour of the financial sector has not changed fundamentally in a number of dimensions since the crisis. While some changes in behaviour are taking place, these are not deep or broad enough. The industry still prizes short-term profit over long-term prudence, today's bonus over tomorrow's relationship. To restore trust, we need a shift toward greater integrity and accountability. We need a stronger and systematic ethical dimension.[9]

Lagarde offers what is almost a definition of the common good as it relates to the goals of financial sector:

> Its goal is to put resources to productive use, to transform maturity, thereby contributing to the good of economic stability and full employment –and ultimately, to the wellbeing of people.

Is Catholic Social Teaching "the better way" that Alan Greenspan dreamed of as he surveyed the wreckage of neoliberalism in the aftermath of 2008? Does this analysis address the flaws in the neoliberal system? Would these reforms restore trust, remove sources of instability, and make businesses more sustainable long-term? Would markets function better? Are the adjustments required in the way business and the economy works feasible and realistic? Are they politically do-able? And more fundamentally, would a post neoliberal market economy as described here make for a fairer, more vibrant and more prosperous economy and a happier and more fulfilled population? We believe we have given adequate grounds for answering all those questions in the affirmative.

chapter 8 – references

1   'Average FTSE 100 CEO is 53-Year-Old Male Accountant' *Management Today* May, 2013.

2   Companies Act 2006, http://www.legislation.gov.uk/ukpga/2006/46/section/172

3   Chris Giles, 'Economists puzzled by Britain's upswing' *Financial Times*, September 2013.

4   Jason Horowitz, 'The Catholic Roots of Obama's Activism' *New York Times* 22 March 2014.

5   Pope Francis, Apostolic Exhortation *Evangelii Gaudium* (2013).

6   KPMG *The Living wage* www.kpmg.com/uk/en/issuesandinsights/articlespublications/pages/living-wage.aspx

7   Matthew Taylor *Getting Engaged* RSA Journal 2013.

8   Christine Lagarde, *Economic Inclusion and Financial Integrity* www.imf.org/external/np/speeches/2014/052714.htm (2014).

9   Ibid.